Cultural Internationalism
and World Order

AKIRA IRIYE

Cultural Internationalism and World Order

The Johns Hopkins University Press

BALTIMORE AND LONDON

© 1997 The Johns Hopkins University Press
All rights reserved. Published 1997
Printed in the United States of America on acid-free paper

06 05 04 03 02 01 00 99 98 97   5 4 3 2 1

The Johns Hopkins University Press
2715 North Charles Street
Baltimore, Maryland 21218-4319
The Johns Hopkins Press Ltd., London

Library of Congress Cataloging-in-Publication Data will be found
at the end of this book.
A catalog record for this book is available from the British Library.

ISBN 0-8018-5457-1

To Maeva Margaret

CONTENTS

Some of the ideas in these essays were first presented in 1988 at the Johns Hopkins University, whose Department of History invited me to present the Albert Shaw Memorial Lectures. Entitled "War and Peace in the Twentieth Century," the lectures sought to trace changing ideas about war and peace from the 1880s to the post-1945 years. Similar but extensively revised lectures were later given at the University of Hawaii, where I had the privilege of serving as a Burns visiting professor in early 1989.

Several years have since elapsed, and in the course of rewriting these pieces for publication, I narrowed the focus considerably. I remain keenly interested in the study of international affairs as an intellectual and cultural phenomenon, of which changing ideas of war and peace are important aspects. But these ideas are so wide-ranging and so intimately linked to the realities of war and peace that to write about them would be tantamount to describing the whole history of international relations. In the intervening years I published studies of United States foreign affairs between the two world wars, post-1945 Japanese foreign relations, and Chinese-Japanese interactions since the late nineteenth century. But I also wanted

to do something different—something more explicitly conceptual, with ideas and cross-national movements, rather than
nations and governments, as principal objects of analysis. I decided to focus on internationalist visions in the twentieth century, especially those that are associated with what I call "cultural internationalism."

In a way, the book looks at one idea of peace: the idea that
world order can and should be defined through interactions
at the cultural level across national boundaries. I hope that
these chapters will indicate the rich legacy of cultural internationalism, something that has tended to be obscured in conventional accounts of international history. As we near the end
of the twentieth century and, as historians, try to make sense
of the forces that have shaped the contemporary world, we
should, I think, pay due attention to themes and visions that,
while not as immediately obvious as geopolitical rivalries, economic development and crises, social upheavals, and a host of
other phenomena, have developed with their own momentum. Indeed, cultural internationalist forces may prove to be a
key factor in defining the world of the next century. But no
historian is comfortable with making speculative statements,
and my interest lies not in predicting the future but in rescuing from scholarly neglect what I believe to have been a persistent theme in twentieth-century history.

Although the original lectures have been considerably revised
with the new focus in mind, I would not have dared to undertake
even this, more modest, attempt if the Johns Hopkins University
had not given me an opportunity for a stimulating exchange
of views. To the members of its history department, and to the
historians at the University of Hawaii, I am deeply indebted.

In 1992 I was honored to be appointed a centennial visiting professor at the London School of Economics. The appointment gave me an excellent opportunity to conduct research and to interact with British historians who shared my interest in modern internationalism. A rough idea of the book took shape then, which was further developed in the spring of 1993, when I was invited to spend several weeks at the Centre d'Etudes Nord-Américaines, Ecole des Hautes Etudes en Sciences Sociales, in Paris. To my hosts at these institutions, especially Ian Nish, D. C. Watt, and Jean Heffer, I owe an enormous personal and professional debt. Needless to say, my colleagues at Harvard University have been a constant source of support and inspiration. I am particularly grateful to John McGreevy, who read a final version of the manuscript and shared with me his insights in the field of modern U.S. religious and intellectual history.

Frank Ninkovich and Robert David Johnson, two leading historians of U.S. internationalism, gave a thorough and encouraging reading to an earlier draft, even as they asked some tough questions. I would also like to record my thanks to Ron Kim, Rani Fedson, Hugh McNeal, Rudolf Janssens, Oliver Schmidt, Harumi Furuya, Steven Schwartzberg, Roman Szporluk, Sadao Asada, and especially to Amnon Finkelstein for providing me with much valuable material that I have taken the liberty to incorporate. At Chicago, Harvard, Paris, London, and elsewhere, I have had the privilege of working with a large number of gifted graduate and undergraduate students whose research in connection with their doctoral dissertations and senior theses has added enormously to my understanding of cultural internationalism. They will be among the next generation's leaders in the study of international history, and I feel confident that many of them will explore in greater depth some of the themes presented in this volume. My wife, Mit-suko, our daughter, Masumi, and her husband, David O'Brien, have tried over the years to help me develop more than a ca-sual familiarity with the world of music, art, and literature even as I talk about the cultural aspects of international rela-tions. They have not thus far succeeded, but I am certain that I would have written a different sort of book without the stimulating environment provided by my family. Finally, to Henry Tom, executive editor at the Johns Hopkins University Press, I would like to express my thanks for waiting so pa-tiently for what I promised I would write many years ago.

Cultural Internationalism and World Order

Introduction

In these essays I have tried to examine the history of international relations since the late nineteenth century not as a story of interactions among sovereign states but in terms of cross-national activities by individuals and groups of people, not always or primarily as representatives of governments but as agents for movements transcending national entities. Individual nations and governments will be mentioned, but I do not undertake a systematic analysis of their policies. This is a study of international relations, but the focus is more on *inter* than on *national*.

The bulk of writings in this field still tends to be presented in the framework of sovereign national entities. As long as such entities exist, that is obviously an acceptable approach; perhaps it is the only plausible starting point. But not all international relations consist of dealings among states and governments, unless one thus defines the subject. Interactions outside these frameworks exist, for which *international relations* may be an inadequate term but which, whatever one calls them, constitute just as much part of the story of world development as do the activities of national entities. I hope the book will show that it is perfectly possible to narrate the drama of international relations without giving principal roles to separate national existences.

One consequence of this approach is to downplay the theme of power. A sovereign nation is by definition held together by a structure of power domestically, and it exists in a geopolitical relationship to other sovereign nations externally. International relations are, at this level of analysis, interpower relations. One tends to emphasize the "great powers" because they, presumably, determine the shape of the world ("world order") at a given moment in time. But the world is created and recreated as much by individuals from "lesser powers" as by the great powers. Who can deny that thinkers, artists, and musicians from small countries have contributed decisively to the making of contemporary history? What does it matter from which country they have come? Their influences have been extensive across national boundaries, and their visions have survived wars and clashes of national interests.

We are, of course, talking about different definitions of the world—indeed, about different worlds. Sometimes they overlap, sometimes they do not. International relations are the sum of all such worlds, and the study of international relations must embrace differently created, postulated, and reconstructed world orders. This book is an attempt to understand one such world order. It argues that individuals and groups of people from different lands have sought to develop an alternative community of nations and peoples on the basis of their cultural interchanges and that, while frequently ridiculed by practitioners of power politics and ignored by historians, their efforts have significantly altered the world community and immeasurably enriched our understanding of international affairs. I call the inspiration behind these endeavors, as well as the sum of their achievements, "cultural internationalism."

Now, neither internationalism nor culture is an uncontroversial concept. In this book the term *internationalism* is used to refer to an idea, a movement, or an institution that seeks to reformulate the nature of relations among nations through cross-national cooperation and interchange. Of course, cooperation and interchange can take place among sovereign states; after all, that is what is meant by "diplomacy." And international cooperation often takes the form of a military alliance, a security treaty, or the like that does not alter the geopolitical character of a given world order. But there is also an internationalism of a different sort, one that aspires to a more peaceful and stable world order through transnational efforts. The chapters in this book cite various examples: legal internationalism, with a stress on international law and arbitration; economic internationalism, envisaging a global network of economic exchanges; and socialist internationalism, promoted by those who believed that world peace must be built upon the solidarity of workers everywhere. Above all, this book delineates the development of cultural internationalism, the fostering of international cooperation through cultural activities across national boundaries.

The term *culture,* too, has been variably defined, making *cultural internationalism* a far from simple or static conception. In this book I adopt the generally accepted definition of culture as "structures of meaning," including "memory, ideology, emotions, life styles, scholarly and artistic works, and other symbols."[1] Cultural internationalism entails a variety of activities undertaken to link countries and peoples through the exchange of ideas and persons, through scholarly cooperation, or through efforts at facilitating cross-national understanding. When Jean-Jacques Rousseau wrote in the mid-eighteenth century that the European states shared "the same religion, the same international law . . . customs, literature, commerce, and . . . a kind of balance of power," he was envisaging a European internationalism defined by culture (religion, law, customs, literature), as well as by economics (commerce) and by power.[2] In addition to religion, law, customs, and literature, many other activities were added to the domain of cultural internationalism in the subsequent periods, as these chapters will show.

Rousseau was referring to a cultural internationalism within the European context. One of the challenges the movement faced, as it gained momentum at the turn of the twentieth century, was to extend itself to other regions and cultures. This was an enormously complex task, and one aim of this book is to describe how each generation sought to cope with the challenge. Here it will be useful to note that even in the West, where modern cultural internationalism originated, the meaning of culture has changed over time. Redefining *culture* has itself been a cultural activity. Cultural internationalism, because it promotes cultural communication and understanding across national boundaries, is inevitably bound up with the notions about culture that prevail in a given time and place.

For instance, during the second half of the nineteenth century, when culture tended primarily to connote scientific research, artistic creation, musical performance, and similar "high" pursuits, there was a growing movement in Europe and North America to encourage scholarly and artistic exchanges among nations as a way to produce a more peaceful world; various international expositions that were held are good examples of this incipient cultural internationalism, which had a cosmopolitan connotation.

By the turn of the century, when the same inspiration produced many world fairs, this "high culture" approach had come to be coupled with, if not eclipsed by, an idea of civilization, which incorporated a whole nation, a whole people; not just elites but the entire population partook of cultural activities because they were members of a civilization. As Frank Ninkovich has shown in his *Modernity and Power*, civilization was equated with order, progress, and modernization.[3] In other words, civilization described what was happening in the West. Cultural internationalism in such a context meant intra-Western exchanges of information and technology; all people, members of the evolving mass societies, could participate. The non-Western world, however, was largely left out of the picture.

This was the very moment, interestingly enough, when some Asian and Middle Eastern peoples began to undertake modernization programs, thereby hoping to elevate themselves to the ranks of civilized nations. Modernization meant Westernization; that is, adopting Western concepts and techniques of modern civilization. The West had to consider whether to welcome such endeavors, and in this connection the racial factor played a crucial role. The European and North American understanding of culture, whether evidenced in popular responses to imperialistic activities in the tropical areas or in scholarly work in the fields of evolutionary biology and anthropology, became heavily intertwined with doctrines of racial differences. Culture and race, in other words, were often interchangeable propositions. In such circumstances, cultural internationalism had to confront the question of allegedly immutable racial distinctions. As chapter 1 of this book shows, the inability to come to grips with the issue was a weakness of pre-World War I cultural internationalism.

Chapters 2 and 3 deal with the decades following World War I.

The racial question remained, but there were significant forces in the 1920s that promoted internationalism across cultural and racial boundaries; or rather, these boundaries were coming down as a result of the universalizing forces of modern communication, transportation, and entertainment. Believing that what he observed in Hawaii was a harbinger of future trends, Robert Park, an American sociologist, confidently predicted that "races and cultures die . . . but civilization lives on."[4] He was reflecting the growing recognition that racial distinctions were less determinative of historical development than had earlier been thought. Although Park still used the terms *race* and *culture* interchangeably, one would no longer assume that racial and cultural diversity was an obstacle to internationalism. Manley O. Hudson, a Harvard law professor, could write of the emergence of "a single world community" in which different peoples would partake of the benefits of civilization equally.[5] Civilization's universalizing force, many even began to argue, could in time obliterate differences among people, or at least make their differences of little consequence in defining the world. If we take all these ideas as manifestations of the culture of the postwar decade, then it seems clear that cultural internationalism was working out a way of solving the race question that had seemed intractable before World War I.

It might be thought, on considering the racialist doctrine of Nazi Germany and other fascist states and the pan-Asianist rhetoric of militarist Japan in the 1930s, that the old definition of culture in terms of racial characteristics came back with a vengeance in reaction to the more universalistic notions of the 1920s. But, without denying German and Japanese racial essentialism—creeds that equated nation with culture and cul-

ture with race—there were other significant developments in
the 1930s, particularly in the democracies. Warren Susman has
shown that the words *the American way of life* gained popular
currency during that decade—a concept that defined a unique
national culture.[6] In this view, race was of far less importance
than history; it was now possible to think that nations interacted with each other through their respective ways of life.
This reconceptualization of culture enabled the democracies
to define their anti-Axis war as a struggle for civilization, now
viewed as the sum of the ways of life of their peoples. Thus,
both in the totalitarian states and in the democracies, national
communities were being viewed as cultures, as webs of meaning, even as the two opposed each other in ideological terms:
antiliberal versus democratic ways of life. The democracies'
victory in World War II meant that certain cultures—more
democratic, more liberal, less racist—would come to shape the
world after the conflict.

In 1943, George Orwell commented: "We live in a lunatic
world in which opposites are constantly changing into one another, in which pacifists find themselves worshipping Hitler,
Socialists become nationalists, patriots become quislings, Bud-
dhists pray for the success of the Japanese army, and the Stock
Market takes an upward turn when the Russians stage an offensive."[7] Here, it might seem, was conceptual confusion. But
along with the paradoxes came undeniable facts: the victory of
the democracies over Germany and Japan and the impetus the
global war gave to nationalistic movements in many colonial
areas. The former suggested that the postwar world would
once again come to embrace the idea of a common humanity;
the latter ensured that this world would be a multicultural
one. Both these developments had important implications for

the development of cultural internationalism. The story is briefly sketched in chapter 4.

By 1945 most racialist doctrines had been cast aside for an attempt at an internationalism free from racial considerations. Culture, to be sure, continued to be seen as a people's way of life, a view attested to by a vogue for "national character" studies such as Ruth Benedict's *Patterns of Culture* and David Potter's *People of Plenty.* The latter was a typical scholarly argument about the U.S. national character. While, after the 1960s, the idea of national character tended to give way to an emphasis on subcultures (or "communities") in some countries, this simply meant that cultural internationalism would now demand a truly global network of communication both across and within national boundaries.

Meantime, decolonization and so-called nation-building in formerly colonial areas were creating new nations (and their respective cultures) and challenging Western-centered cultural formulations. These forces pushed for multiculturalist agendas, as did various ethnic and religious groups within national communities. In such a multicultural world, there was an inevitable tendency toward essentialism—the view that every culture is unique, making significant communication among cultures difficult—a development that could be checked only by a cultural internationalism of a new variety. Now the emphasis would be on not just mutual cultural understanding but on cross-cultural cooperation to deal with global issues such as environmental degradation, human rights, and demographic explosion.

At the same time, however, after World War II culture also came to be seen in the context of social transformation. This was a new problematique, emerging in the wake of the war:

cultural change as an aspect of, or an agency of, not just modernization but also the internationalization of nations. That cultures *could* change was an assumption underlying the allied occupation of Germany, Japan, and other countries. Reinhold Wagnleitner has documented the "Coca-Colonization" of Austrian society and culture after 1945.[8] It was not just that Austrian ways of life and habits of thought began to change, but also that these changes linked the country to others that were undergoing similar transformations. A young U.S. lawyer overseeing educational reforms in occupied Japan reported as early as the fall of 1946 that he had "already attended an opera and two concerts by the Nippon Philharmonic Orchestra."[9] Very soon, Japanese musicians would be transforming the artistic landscape not only of their country but throughout the world. The postwar multicultural world, then, was also an intercultural community in which cultural differences and cultural changes proceeded simultaneously, further enriching the vocabulary of cultural internationalism.

The above sketch suggests that cultural internationalism has had an inner history, a product of the changing discourse on the concept of culture. While keeping in view various formulations of culture, this book also considers cultural internationalism *externally;* that is, in relation to other definitions of international relations, of which, as noted at the outset, the geopolitical one has been the most influential.

The dialectic between cultural internationalism and geopolitical realism (i.e., the view that power is the only reality that counts) is conceptually akin to the dichotomy between idealism and realism; but in the following chapters I suggest that the two are not static and that in many ways cultural internationalists have viewed themselves as realists, comprehending the deeper springs of human intellect and emotions as a more solid basis than armaments and collective national interests on which to build a stable world community. Starting in the years before World War I, the exponents of cultural internationalism believed that theirs was not a naive vision of a utopian community but a realistic proposal for avoiding nationalistic excesses. Their voices were drowned out by calls for more arms and for war, but the tragedy made the postwar internationalists all the more determined to push for a cultural definition of international affairs.

In many ways, the years between the two world wars saw a serious dialogue between cultural internationalism and geopolitical realism. The former was exemplified by League of Nations programs that that organization called "intellectual cooperation" across national boundaries; the latter was promoted by war planners in various countries who were never convinced that the Great War—World War I—had changed anything. The dialogue came down to the contest between cultural and military forces, between culture and power, for ordering the postwar world. Culture seemed to gain ascendancy throughout the 1920s, as military force was reduced in many countries and as individuals crossed national boundaries not as soldiers but as students, tourists, and literary exiles. The situation was reversed in the following decade, but it would be too simplistic to say that the rise of totalitarianism and the aggressive wars launched by Germany, Japan, and their allies amounted to the victory of geopolitics and the defeat of cultural internationalism. As chapter 3 notes, the latter asserted itself time and again, even in the environment of violence and intolerance. Besides, it is possible to argue that the almost suicidal decisions by the Nazi and Japanese leaders to take on the world was, in a perverted fashion, nothing less than the triumph of culture over power. It then took the allies' power to destroy Axis culture.

The dialogue between power and culture survived World War II. The Cold War was, at one level, clearly a geopolitical confrontation between the nuclear superpowers, dividing the world into two competing alliance systems. But it was also an ideological contest, and here the superiority of one side was evident, even at the beginning and certainly by the end of the cold war. U.S. ideas and ways of life were far more influential than their Soviet counterpart, so the geopolitical struggle always existed in juxtaposition with the Americanization of the world. That process had begun much earlier, and in the absence of the cold war it might have been even more extensive, or it might not have been. U.S. power may, or may not, have served to promote its cultural hegemony overseas. When the situation is put this way, one notices a unique relationship of power and culture in postwar global affairs. However we answer these hypothetical questions, it is undeniable that cultural internationalism developed with its own momentum to such an extent that it survived the vicissitudes of the cold war and indeed emerged as a significant force for reshaping world order when the cold war ended.

Power, Thomas Hobbes wrote, was "man's present means to obtain some future apparent need."[10] This is a classic statement of the relationship between means and ends. The equation can be used to describe foreign affairs, in the traditional framework, as a quest for attaining national interests. The Hobbesian formula can also be utilized for a discussion of power and culture, because the definition of *some future apparent need* is ultimately a cultural issue. *Culture* determines what the ends of a nation are; *power* provides the means for obtaining them.

Cultural internationalists, however, have argued that even the means should be culturally constructed. They have defined international relations in cultural terms and insisted that cultural means must be employed in such an environment. Even with respect to traditional issues (national security, foreign trade and so forth) cultural internationalism has proposed conceptions in which these become culturally formulated. Both power and culture presuppose order, domestically and internationally; to the extent that the search for order is an end sought by nations, exponents of cultural internationalism would argue, power and culture should not be mutually incompatible means. Rather, both should be used to save humanity from chaos. At the end of the twentieth century, however, the limits of power, whether it be nuclear weapons or localized police force, are quite evident. If power alone cannot maintain order, culture must assume an increasing measure of responsibility. Hobbes's definition of power must become a definition of culture. The history of cultural internationalism during the last century, outlined in the following chapters, gives some hope that cultural forces may indeed be ready for the task.

CHAPTER ONE

The Internationalist Imagination

Cultural internationalism emerged as a significant force in international relations in the late nineteenth and early twentieth centuries in response to the seemingly endless preoccupation of the great powers with military strengthening and colonial domination. Although these decades are usually treated as a prelude to World War I, to which such a preoccupation inevitably led, it is also possible to give them a different reading: they can be seen as an introductory chapter in the history of modern internationalism.

Small incidents often conceal major themes at crucial points in history. The Balkan war of 1912 provides a good example: Leon Trotsky, one of the most astute observers of international affairs, was in Belgrade that summer when the government of Serbia undertook a full mobilization of reservists. His observations on the crisis serve as an excellent point of departure for our discussion of twentieth-century internationalism. What struck him was the pervasive war frenzy in which national, ethnic, and religious groups seemed to be enveloped, even though they all realized the immense destructiveness of military conflict.

"When I learned," he reported, "that some men whom I

knew well—politicians, editors, university teachers—were already under arms, at the frontier, in the front line, that they would be among the first to kill and to be killed—then the war, the abstraction about which I had been speculating so easily in my thoughts and in my articles, seemed to me something utterly unlikely and impossible." He had condemned the Russo-Japanese War as one involving the two armies' chauvinism, arguing that in each country the army was an instrument of domestic repression, "an artificially trained unit, armed against the people." And he had written sarcastically of the German military who, in his words, praised war "as an element of order established by God, or a school of bravery and unselfishness, devotion to duty and self-sacrifice." But the Balkan war made him realize that not just the military but civilian leaders and apparently the entire population craved war. As the Serbian minister of finance told Trotsky, "War? Of course we are against it. Who does not appreciate the advantages of peace? Peace means work, accumulation of wealth, culture"; but peace "as it exists in the Balkans means constant local wars of attrition." This was so particularly because, the Serbian said, "the Muslims are totally incapable of creating conditions for peaceful coexistence with the Christian peoples inhabiting the Turkish Empire." After spending a few weeks in the Balkans and talking to many people, Trotsky concluded that, despite all talk of human progress, "we have not yet crept out on all fours from the barbaric period of our history. We have learned how to wear suspenders, to write clever leading articles, and to make milk chocolate, but when we need to reach a serious decision about how a few different tribes are to live together on a well-endowed European peninsula, we are incapable of finding any other method than mutual extermination on a mass scale."[1]

Five years later, in the middle of a European war that had erupted as if to prove Trotsky's thesis, he was struck by another theme. He noted that the "core of patriotic feeling and military discipline has become as thin as possible" and that all governments now wanted peace. Moreover, the war had raised "to new heights the feeling of 'universality,' of awareness of the indissoluble tie between the fate of an individual and the fate of all mankind."[2] From that awareness, Trotsky believed, forces could develop that would forever banish excessive nationalisms and usher in a new period of international order.

The power of excessive nationalism and visions of international order: this dichotomy has been a defining characteristic of the contemporary world. The dialectic between forces of particularism and universalism has existed throughout history, but in the twentieth century particularly it has been crucial to the understanding of international relations. In a sense, the dichotomy is part of the larger human dialectic between pessimism and optimism, between chaos and order, between power and culture, and between "the realities" and ideals. It is important to note that these pairs are not complete opposites; frequently, for instance, "the realities" of nationalism and war produce novel visions of peace and civilization, and these latter may become incorporated into the new "realities." It is the interplay of these forces on the international stage that is the subject of this study.

Because most studies of international relations focus on national interests, national strategies, national rivalries, nationalistic emotions, and the like, it seems justifiable to trace the evolution of ideas and movements that have sought to develop alternative definitions of world affairs. Among the most potent of these definitions have been a number of internationalist schemes—reformulations of foreign and domestic policies in such a way as to overcome excessive parochialism, with its suspicion and hatred of "the other," and to establish a more interdependent, cooperative, and mutually tolerant international community.

Such visions of international community may be termed *internationalism* to oppose them to forces of nationalism. The latter have been by far the more influential and pervasive "realities" for more than three centuries, but internationalism has also gained strength, if not consistently then at least as an expression of hope on the part of an increasing number of people everywhere. To the extent that a nation is an "imagined community," as Benedict Anderson has argued, the international community must also be "imagined." (Some writers find the term "imagining" too tame and use "inventing" instead: as, for instance, Declan Kiberd does in *Inventing Ireland*.)[3] All the same, the internationalist imagination has exerted a significant influence in modern world history. But the imagination has taken different forms in different periods of time, and the main purpose of this book is to trace various conceptions of international order, with particular emphasis on cultural themes underlying internationalist visions. No attempt is made to be comprehensive; rather, I shall try to describe themes and emphases that have characterized the ideas and practice of internationalism since the nineteenth century.

The polarity of nationalism and internationalism was particularly marked in the decades preceding World War I, when war and peace appeared to hang in a balance and when many internationalist proposals were put forward as alternatives to nationalistic rivalries. In the 1860s, Henry Thomas Buckle had written that, whereas "the actions of men respecting war" had

changed over time, their "moral knowledge respecting it" had
not. Nevertheless, he was confident that wars were "becoming
less frequent." At least until the Crimean War, he noted, "we
had remained at peace for nearly forty years: a circumstance unparalleled not only in our own country, but also in the annals
of every other country which has been important enough to
play a leading part in the affairs of the world."[4] Half a century
later, most observers agreed that "moral knowledge" concerning war derived overwhelmingly from modern nationalism. As
a Serbian journalist told Trotsky in 1912, "what is at stake here
really is our right to live and to develop. The people cannot but
know and feel that without war there is for them no way out
of the blind alley Serbia is in. The people want war."[5] Contrast
this with Jean-Jacques Rousseau's well-known dictum that war
"is a relation . . . between State and State, and individuals are
enemies . . . as soldiers; not as members of their country, but
as its defenders."[6]

During the heyday of Victorian liberalism, such a distinction could be accepted. Immanuel Kant's view that war was
characteristic of arbitrary government and that peace was
characteristic of a constitutional republic gained influence, as
did the Manchester liberals' supposition that the commercial
classes desired peace across national frontiers.[7] Increasingly,
however, such optimism had to confront the realities of aroused
nationalisms. The Rousseauian distinction between state and
nation was challenged by Lord Acton as early as the 1860s,
when he noted that nationality was a force of growing importance in Europe, destabilizing interstate affairs and enhancing
the chances for war. Acton traced this new development to the
French Revolution, which had produced the first modern wars
in the sense of wars fought by the masses imbued with nation-

alism.[8] The idea that ordinary people could unite in the name of their nationality and organize their own country was abhorrent to Acton, but he readily admitted that this was the trend throughout Europe. He saw this modern nationalism as a force against international order.

Clearly, Acton rather than Buckle was the more accurate prophet of the world to come. Nationalism would prove to be the most decisive force in international affairs to such an extent that it came to be equated with military power and with war. As the world was seen to consist of sovereign national entities, whose number appeared destined to grow, the chances for armed conflict could easily be considered to be increasing. As Michael Howard has noted, in prewar Europe nationalism was "almost invariably characterized by militarism." This militarism, he writes, was reinforced by an educational system whose aim "was to produce generations physically fit for and psychologically attuned to war."[9]

All this is clear and points to the daunting task undertaken by those who sought to do something to mitigate forces of nationalism so as to produce a less warlike international environment. Because nationalism was recognized as the key to international tensions, its opposite, internationalism, had to be strengthened if the trend were to be checked. The parallel development of nationalism and internationalism thus makes a fascinating chapter in the story leading up to World War I. Just as nationalism and war were imagined to be interchangeable, internationalists assumed peace was possible only if the forces of internationalism could be strengthened.

Internationalism, of course, existed long before the nineteenth century. The idea of international community developed in parallel with the growth of the nation-state in modern

Europe. It is useful to recall that the emergence of secular sovereign states in the seventeenth century, out of the universalism defined by the Christian church, created a new universalism in the form of international law. There could be no international law without nations, but at the same time it was assumed that the existence of independent states necessitated the definition of a larger community, *magna civitas,* of which the states were members. They would be governed by certain rules and precepts of the community, and these would take precedence over the laws of individual states. Thus, international law was built upon internationalist assumptions. As developed initially by such jurists as Hugo Grotius and Christian Wolff, there was a congruence between the laws of nations and the laws of nature. Both were universalistic in character and could be comprehended by rational faculties. It is true that international law was more often than not honored in the breach, and after the eighteenth century writers came to distinguish the behavior of nations from natural laws and ethical precepts. Moreover, the concept of international law came to lose its universalistic connotations after the eighteenth century and became interchangeable with the European community of nations. Europe, wrote Emerick de Vattel in 1758, was "a sort of republic, whose members—each independent, but all bound together by a common interest—unite for the maintenance of order and the preservation of liberty."[10]

Internationalism in Europe, then, had developed both as a universalistic doctrine, inspired by the concept of natural law, and as a particularistic conception, privileging the European states among nations and empires. By the nineteenth century, international law, having survived numerous wars among European (and North American) states, came to be equated with norms and procedures governing the conduct of "civilized" nations. Among "civilized" nations, it was widely held in Europe and North America, it should be possible to codify laws defining the acceptable behavior of governments and individuals, in war as well as in peace. As Henry Wheaton, American diplomat and jurist, wrote in his influential *Elements of International Law,* first published in 1836, "civilized nations" adhered to certain rules of conduct that they deduced "from the nature of the society existing among independent nations."[11] Those states and peoples that did not accept the laws were by definition "uncivilized"; by the same token, "uncivilized" countries would become "civilized" only by adhering to the existing international law. The Ottoman Empire was admitted to the "civilized" community of nations when it signed treaties with the Western powers in the aftermath of the Crimean War, as were China, Japan, Siam, and Korea, which established formal diplomatic relations with these powers throughout the course of the nineteenth century. Even so, these non-Western countries were not exactly equal members of the "civilized" community of nations: "unequal" treaties continued to function between these two sets of nations.

What is important in our discussion, however, is the fact that even as Turkey, China, Japan, and other countries struggled to become modern states, they were drawn into the system of laws that had been established by Western nations. In other words, these non-Western countries had to embrace both nationalism (imagining themselves to be modern nation-states) and internationalism (visualizing themselves as members of the world community) as they sought to transform themselves. It is interesting to note that several non-Western countries, including Persia, Siam, China, and Japan, were represented at the Hague conference of 1899, convened to modify and strengthen international law.

That conference was a landmark in that it established the first international court of arbitration. Such an undertaking was grounded on the assumption that it was possible for modern nations to cooperate with one another in the international sphere and to agree among themselves to solve their disputes through arbitration, not war. That disputes could be peacefully arbitrated was, of course, an optimistic presupposition that proved premature, but the optimism was a necessary antidote to the prevailing nationalism of the age, by which the great powers were trying to strengthen themselves further through armament. Even as they did so, they were willing to enter into various arbitration agreements. Many of these were signed after the turn of the century, indicating the awareness that, just as nationalism was interchangeable with war, internationalism was an essential condition for the avoidance of war.

How to strengthen forces for internationalism at a time when nationalism appeared to be growing stronger by the day? International law and arbitration was one answer, but internationalists did not stop there. They proposed additional programs and movements. Some offered radical solutions, extending the logic of the nationalism-internationalism polarity by calling for severe restrictions on the rights of sovereign nations and for the organizing of an international regime with authority to maintain the peace. In 1895, Urbain Gohier, who was beginning his long and controversial career as a Paris journalist, published his essay "On War," which argued that wars were advocated by (because they benefited them) dynasties, governments, politicians, large financial organs, capitalists, arms manufacturers, and the military. These entities would go to war in the name of *patrie* and honor, but these were mere words to hide their self-interests. "Our patriotism should consist in working for the well-being of our citizens, not in killing them in order to bring about [their rulers'] well-being." Militarism would bring ruin to the people, and war would cause oppression and servitude in the country. "War is the extreme expression of violence and injustice," and the French nation had established a militaristic regime "for having loved war too much." War created the pretext for "maximum government," whereas justice and well-being required "minimum government." But given the growing power of the state, war could be prevented only if common people, representing "human conscience," rose against war-making leaders. War would cease when would-be war makers recognized that their own lives depended on the support of ordinary people.[12]

Ultimately, however, no amount of domestic reform would suffice unless efforts were made to strengthen the forces for internationalism. Gohier argued that since war was an expression of nationalism, peace would prevail only when nationalism was moderated, if not replaced, by internationalism. And this could be done through coalescing various peoples in a joint effort at international organization. Although he was vague as to details, Gohier was convinced that possibilities existed for developing a world government, embracing at least the civilized peoples, and pointed to the example of the United States. After five months of touring the country, he published a book entitled *The People of the Twentieth Century in the United States* (1903); the American people would dominate the world in the new century, he declared, because of their abundant natural resources, political institutions, republican instincts, and audacious practices of extreme liberty. Europeans would do well to realize that people's liberty in all forms and their initiatives in all degrees were the two factors that made for wealth and civil peace. What struck Gohier above all was that the United States, despite its appearance of "nationalism, particularism, and jingoism," was actually a "splendid example of internationalism." This was because Americans were heirs to all that Europe had produced, without, however, having transported Europe's nationalistic rivalries. "This fusion of European races in America justifies all the doctrines of internationalists who are denounced by mendacious governments and attacked by stupid savants. The American nation is the living realization of the dream of internationalism." Why would the same people, who would be engaged in a fratricide if they fought in the United States, still go to war on the European continent? "We want peace and a close unity between Europeans in Europe and Europeans in the United States. This is the first article of internationalism." Gohier was mindful of the Spanish-American War and the U.S. annexation of the Philippines and warned that if imperialism should turn the United States into a militaristic nation, it would be a disaster for the whole of mankind. Fundamentally, however, he remained hopeful that the more internationalist side of the United States would prevail and lead the world to peace.[13] It would point the way to organizing the nations of the world better for mutual cooperation and peace.

Gustave Hervé, another French writer, established an even more explicit connection between peace and internationalism. In a 1910 book entitled *Internationalism,* he argued that modern states such as France and Germany were temporary and inferior forms of human association that were steadily being undermined by forces of internationalism; namely, the movement of people, goods, and capital across national frontiers. Internationalism, he asserted, "is nothing but an instinctive or reflective aspiration of the modern world for political forms superior to the actual states" so that the whole of humanity could live as in one country covering the entire earth—*la grande patrie universelle*. This was an inevitable historical evolution, starting with the Protestants helping one another across national boundaries and the French Revolution's universalistic doctrines. Like Gohier, Hervé gave credit to the United States, which, he wrote, had established the idea of humanity as one family of which all members shared the same rights.

In the second half of the nineteenth century, Hervé maintained, the development of modern science and technology had made "historically determined political frontiers appear anachronistic." There had developed an internationalism of capital and labor, neither of which knew political boundaries. As capital and labor continued to cross frontiers, the distinction between domestic and foreign goods and populations would diminish, and international regulations would be promulgated to govern their behavior. Capitalists and workers, thus internationalized, would try to avoid disastrous economic competition as well as "the most disastrous of all competitions, war." Although at that moment the chances of war or peace appeared evenly balanced, the latter would be the ultimate winner, especially since the world's working class wanted it. "The nineteenth century was a century of nationalism," Hervé asserted, "but the twentieth century will be a century of internationalism. . . . There will eventually be a United States of Europe and America, perhaps a United States of the world." The book concluded with a ringing declaration: "Future generations will marvel that at the beginning of the twentieth

century, barbarism had divided the world into small compart-
ments filled with bayonets and cannons, that they would destroy one another at the order of their masters, and that those
who dared to speak of the end of this barbarism were considered fools and public misfits."[14]

Hervé's conviction that capital and labor were tending toward internationalization echoed widespread ideas in the second half of the nineteenth century and the first years of the
twentieth that economics was prevailing over politics. Against
the all too apparent tendency of modern nation-states to arm
themselves in preparation for war against one another, many
assumed that the best way to combat this trend was through
encouraging economic activities across national boundaries. If
carried out unfettered, such activity would inevitably weaken
the forces of nationalism. This idea, that economic transactions would strengthen interdependence and peaceful relations among nations, may be termed *economic internationalism*, in contrast to *legal internationalism*. The latter stressed
legal agreements and institutions for the sustenance of an international community, whereas the former saw the answer to
modern national antagonisms in international commerce and
worldwide economic development.

The origins of modern economic internationalism go back
to the eighteenth century, when Enlightenment thinkers and
officials began challenging the theories and practices of mer-
cantilism and argued that increased commercial transactions
benefited all nations. Some went further and conceptualized a
vision of international relations in which there was an inherent
connection between trade and cross-national understanding,
and between cross-national understanding and world peace.
As Joseph Priestley wrote, "by commerce we enlarge our ac-

quaintance with the terraqueous globe and its inhabitants, which tends greatly to expand the mind, and to cure us of many hurtful prejudices, which we unavoidably contract in a confined situation at home. . . . [No] person can take the sweets of commerce, which absolutely depends upon a free and undisturbed intercourse of different and remote nations, but must grow fond of peace, in which alone the advantages he enjoys can be had."[15] Such a conception of economic internationalism was given additional theoretical underpinnings in the nineteenth century, as world trade expanded in the wake of the Congress of Vienna and brought peoples and their products closer together. Perhaps the best-known writer in this regard was the sociologist Herbert Spencer, whose 1876 *Principles of Sociology* was enormously influential. In this volume, Spencer sought to trace the evolution of human societies, from the isolated primitive communities to organizations dominated by the military in order to ensure collective survival and territorial expansion, and to modern industrial nations whose primary function was to undertake economic development. In these latter, "civilized," societies, human activities not directly linked to military affairs and therefore pursued by private individuals and groups were constantly being enlarged. As a result, interconnections among nations in a similar stage of development would grow, which ultimately would bring them closer to the ideal of universal peace.[16]

Already in such thinking one notes an interest in social and cultural, not just economic, aspects of international relations. For what Priestley, Spencer, and others were presenting was a vision of an international community in which nations and peoples gained a more mature understanding of one another than had been possible when commerce was combined with military conquest and seen in terms of sovereign states' struggles for power. Distant parts of the world were being brought closer together through modern shipping, trade, and marketing organizations, and it seemed possible to expect the growth of mutual knowledge and, as a result, a greater sense of shared concerns and interests across national boundaries. This additional element in internationalist thought may be termed *cultural internationalism;* that is, the idea that internationalism may best be fostered through cross-national cultural communication, understanding, and cooperation. A more peaceful world order could develop not just through the drafting of legal documents, the establishment of international courts, or engagement in unrestricted commerce, but through the efforts of individuals and organizations across national boundaries to promote better understanding and to cooperate in collaborative enterprises. Such ideas significantly enriched, even transformed, modern internationalism. Any conception of world order or international community would now have to contain all elements: legal, economic, and cultural.

This last element, the cultural, emerged as a major characteristic of twentieth-century internationalism. It is an important phenomenon. In this book, particular attention is paid to the development of cultural internationalism as a key aspect of modern efforts and movements to realize a more humane, peaceful world.

It was not surprising that cultural internationalism emerged in the last decades of the nineteenth and the first decades of the twentieth centuries, as if to challenge the growing tides of nationalism and militarism. In confronting the realities of armed rivalries and geopolitical calculations that were then dominating international relations, internationalists felt the need for cross-national efforts to keep alive the vision of an interdependent world community. The new internationalism in the age of the new imperialism thus inevitably called for cooperative undertakings among nations to promote a sense of global interdependence. More specifically, officials and intellectual leaders in various countries became strongly interested in establishing international organizations for carrying out joint cultural projects. H. L. S. Lyons notes in his pioneering study *Internationalism in Europe* (1963) that more than four hundred international organizations had been established prior to World War I, ranging from the Red Cross to associations of scientists and doctors, all dedicated to the proposition that such organizations would promote interdependence and peace. For instance, in 1885 an International Institute of Statistics was founded to standardize national statistical information. Two years later, an international bureau was established to collect and publish tariffs of many countries. These instances were in effect attempts at internationalizing national data, an idea that was also behind such other examples as the Universal Postal Union and an international agreement on standards of weights and measures. Lyons shows that the bulk of these organizations came into being after the 1870s—an indication that they were responses to the growing nationalism and militarization of the age.[17]

It is true that the majority of these institutions were functional, in the sense of having been created in order to serve specific purposes such as establishing international postal rates or collecting customs information. Some may argue that these devices merely facilitated the execution of national policies and that whatever cultural internationalist ideas these institutions may have implied were of secondary importance. Never-

theless, such modest beginnings in the functional sphere provided evidence that, even as the nations of the world were
turning themselves into military powers, it was possible to
achieve cross-national cooperation and establish international
structures. These agencies could, and did, stimulate and encourage cultural internationalist thought.

A good example is a remarkably prescient book published
by Leonard Woolf in 1916, *International Government*. Woolf
took note of the mushrooming of these institutions and put
them in the Spencerian context of the development of modern
civilization, arguing that international organizations were indeed part of a significant trend of modern history. Human affairs were becoming less and less confined to national boundaries, and fewer and fewer problems were susceptible of
solution within a national framework. That Woolf was by no
means alone in such a view may be seen in Friedrich Naumann's *Mitteleuropa*, published in 1915, in which Naumann, a
member of the Reichstag, traced the development of "the international idea" and postulated the evolution of human organizations from family to tribe to nation to superstate province.
Woolf cited such organizations as an international literary and
artistic association and a congress of directors of astronomical
observatories to demonstrate how far international relations
had progressed in promoting internationalism. He might have
added several international women's organizations that had
begun to be established at the end of the nineteenth century.[18]
These examples were far more than functional bodies, and
they indicated the emergence of a culturally defined internationalist movement.

The movement was abetted by numerous international conferences and symposia, bringing together scholars, religious

leaders, artists, and others from various parts of the world. It is interesting to note that many of these conferences were held in conjunction with international exhibitions, or world's fairs, one of the earliest examples being the Parliament of Religions held in Chicago in 1893 to coincide with the Columbian Exposition. Lyons notes that forty-two such exhibitions, often called expositions, were held between 1851 and 1914. Initially intended for the showing and marketing of manufactured products, the fairs soon came to include the exhibition of traditional cultural wares from different countries—an indication that economic internationalism was blending with an interest in promoting cross-cultural understanding. Moreover, as John MacKenzie has noted, these fairs were often housed in buildings in the "Oriental" style, a sure sign that, however superficial, there was an awareness of the interconnectedness of various cultures.[19]

The Chicago Parliament of Religions was one of the first instances of an explicitly cultural formulation of internationalism. The world's cultural (in this instance, religious) leaders were brought together for an exchange of information and ideas. They shared the conviction that the time was ripe for such an undertaking, that through direct personal contact and communication, the participants would not only gain an understanding of other faiths and philosophies but would collectively contribute to the making of a more interdependent community of nations and peoples.

Also in 1893, an international congress of anthropology was held in the same city. International congresses of scholars were in fact becoming frequent occurrences. As early as 1869, the first "international congress of anthropology and prehistorical archaeology" had been convened in Copenhagen, and similar gatherings had been organized in fields ranging from "archaeology and history" to "applied chemistry." Calling them "international congresses" (although, as will be noted, "international" meant primarily European and North American) reflected the growing sentiment among intellectuals that they could make a contribution to the world community by "developing international ties," as a participant in the 1898 "international congress of historical sciences," convened in the Hague, pointed out. To take another example, at the Paris Universal Exposition, held in 1900, there was much excitement over Esperanto, an international language developed by Ludwik Zamenhof, whose first textbook, *International Language*, had been published in 1887. Many French intellectuals embraced the Esperanto movement, and in 1905 the first congress was convened in Paris. The tenth congress, also in Paris, held on August 1, 1914, was attended by four thousand representatives—a testimony to the still persistent force of cultural internationalism on the very eve of the intra-European war. (It was reported that some years before the war, German and British unionists had communicated with each other in Esperanto, and that in 1911-12, and even during World War I, Social Democrats in Sweden voted in favor of Esperanto as a second language.)[20]

On a more massive scale, international expositions such as the 1904 St. Louis World's Fair and the one in San Francisco eleven years later promoted the goal of cross-cultural communication. In St. Louis, the International Congress of Arts and Science was held alongside the exposition, and a large number of the world's leading scientists, literary figures, and scholars representing many fields of the humanities and the social sciences presented retrospective looks at the cultural achievements of the nineteenth century and predicted future developments. In San Francisco, the fair celebrated the opening of the Panama Canal. While there was undoubted U.S. nationalistic pride at this technological feat, which had obvious military and strategic implications, the fair's organizers stressed that the canal was a human, not just an American, achievement and held immense potentialities as a highway of peaceful intercourse among nations.[21]

One of the most interesting developments in this context was the establishment in Brussels, in 1910, of a Union des Associations Internationales. Its purpose was to serve as the headquarters for 132 cross-national organizations. The union's publication, *La vie internationale,* opened its first issue with a ringing endorsement of "the vast movement of ideas, facts, and organizations that constitute the international life" and declared that "the international progress of humanity" was now irresistible. Not that nations were going to disappear; the editors took pains to point out that internationalism was not incompatible with nationalism, but that the internationalists recognized these trends and were committed to promoting "entente, concord, and cooperation" among nations. In a revealing essay in this issue, Henri La Fontaine and Paul Otlet, prominent Belgian internationalists, wrote that the movement for organizing international life incorporated, but went much beyond, international law, pacifism, or political internationalism. The new internationalism was more comprehensive than any of these particular movements and considered the "interests, ideals, and hopes of humanity and of the whole world."[22] Here clearly was a vision of an international community of shared interests and ideals, an imagined world order in which these interests and ideals would overcome differences and antagonisms among nations.

These were the expressions of prewar liberal internationalism. A more radical variety was promoted by socialists, Marxists, and others willing to go a step further and argue that a world order of peace and justice could be achieved only when workers united across nations and put an end to the state systems that oppressed them. As James Joll, W. B. Gallie, and others have shown, radical thinkers in the Marxist tradition were not necessarily opposed to all wars; some, notably Friedrich Engels, argued that wars among capitalist states could even be welcomed by workers, as a catalyst that might enable them to seize power in the anticipated aftermath of destruction and chaos.[23] The radicals in many instances preferred such wars to a capitalist-defined peace that, many of them asserted, perpetuated the oppression of workers. On the other hand, the radicals were adamantly opposed to militarism, imperialism, and other programs for the strengthening of the state, and called upon the proletariat of all countries to resist them. The Amsterdam meeting of Russian and Japanese socialists in 1905, to declare their opposition to the war going on between the two countries, was a good example.

Just as liberal internationalists were convinced of the need to establish worldwide organizations to promote their cause, radicals created their own institution, the International Workingmen's Association, which was intended to serve the interests of workers throughout the world for a just peace—a peace not for perpetuating capitalist domination but for enhancing the dignity and well-being of ordinary people. Commonly known as the Second International (the First International Workingmen's Association, founded by Karl Marx in 1864, had been wrecked by internal ideological dissension), the organization, established in 1889 with its headquarters in Brussels, spread the Marxist perspective on proletarian solidarity across national frontiers: as Benito Mussolini asserted in 1910, not "bourgeois and democratic pacifism" but "only internationalistic socialism" would prevent war.[24]

Socialist internationalism was not necessarily the same thing as cultural internationalism, any more than business internationalism was. Both proletarian and capitalist internationalists had functional agendas, like the promotion of an alternative domestic political order or of international trade. Nevertheless, one should note the cultural implications of socialist internationalism, because, as Sondra Herman has argued, it was communitarian in that it was grounded on a view of humanity that preceded the existence of states. Like Gohier and Hervé, but going a step beyond their argument, Jane Addams, the foremost communitarian internationalist in the United States, asserted that internationalism was ultimately incompatible with modern nationalism, and that only by coalescing the aspirations of voiceless, powerless masses everywhere could there emerge a truly interdependent and peaceful world.[25] Although the Socialist International may have been "an aspiration not a reality," as Mussolini said in 1914, and although it was far more influential in Europe than in North America, such views suggest that throughout the Western world socialist internationalism was developing in parallel with liberal capitalist internationalism.[26]

How about the non-Western world? It was noted earlier that internationalism had its origins in seventeenth-century Europe but that its application in the form of international law came to be limited to Western nations. Eméric Crucé, a French writer, may have been one of the first exceptions in this regard when he argued, in his book *Nouveau Cynée* (1623) that "human society is a body all of whose members have a common sympathy" and that international agreements should be viewed as universally applicable, being "useful to all nations alike and agreeable to those that have some ray of reason and sentiment of humanity." He proposed the establishment of an international court of arbitration to be situated in Venice and represented by Persia, China, Japan, Ethiopia, Morocco, the Mogul empire, and the East and West Indies, in addition to the countries of Europe.[27] Remarkable as such a proposal was, it would be more than two centuries before it was put into practice. In an ironical twist of history, it seems that internationalism as a theory and practice became narrower in the eighteenth and nineteenth centuries, insofar as the non-Western parts of the world were concerned, even as technological developments were bringing all peoples of the globe into closer contact, so that in its nineteenth- and early twentieth-century variety, internationalism conceptualized a world of interdependence primarily among "civilized" peoples.

What, then, about peoples not considered "civilized"? Who were the "civilized"? In terms of international law, as seen above, such countries as Turkey, China, Japan, Korea, and Siam had been steadily incorporated into the "civilized" community of nations. Latin American countries, of course, had been viewed as members of this community as soon as their independence was recognized. Nevertheless, internationalist thought, whether of capitalist or socialist variety, tended primarily to embrace the European and North American nations. This was fundamentally because the countries outside Europe and North America had been technologically and economically outdistanced by the West; hence, neither capitalism nor socialism would be a useful concept to apply to them. But there was also the overall assumption that world affairs were dominated by the Western powers and that, even as their militarism and preparedness for war were being decried by the internationalists, few, if any, considered the alternative of redefining world order by incorporating the less powerful and less developed. As late as 1894, when war broke out between China and Japan, observers in Europe initially dismissed it as of little consequence, since neither combatant was a "civilized" power.[28] It was not really a war as defined by "civilized" international law. The situation did not really change in the wake of the Sino-Japanese War, even though Japan's victory turned it into one of the "civilized" powers. Japanese officials and propagandists had, in fact, touted during the war that this was a struggle for civilization; that Japan was trying to combat the reactionary traditionalism of China and Korea. Whether they succeeded in convincing Europeans and North Americans, or indeed Asians and even themselves, that Japan was more "civilized" than China and Korea was less important than that civilization in international relations was equated, once again, with military power so that Japan's victory entitled it to claim the new status. Within a few years, the nation was indeed joining the other "civilized" powers in sending an expedition to China to suppress the Boxers, who were viewed as enemies of civilization.

Military power was one thing. Did Japan's joining the West as a "civilized" power make a difference in internationalist movements? After all, here was, for the first time, a non-Western country joining the Western-dominated community of nations. Various forces were agitating in Europe and North America to push their nations away from militarism and geopolitics. Were similar forces at work in Japan? How did its emergence as a military power affect the various notions of internationalism?

In the cultural sphere, modest but important developments were evident. Although "international" or "world" congresses and conferences always consisted overwhelmingly of Europeans and North Americans, a few Japanese began to be invited. It is interesting to note that the membership list of the 1898 congress of historians, held in the Hague and attended by more than three hundred participants, contained four Japanese names but none from other non-Western parts of the world. The Japanese foreign minister even served as one of the honorary chairmen of the conference, indicating an eagerness to be associated with "the great task" of building intellectual ties with Westerners. Six years later, at the St. Louis International Congress of Arts and Science, four speakers from Japan joined scores of prominent scholars, artists, and literary figures in making presentations: two scientists, one art historian (Okakura Kakuzō), and one jurist. Inasmuch as there was no one else from Asia, the Japanese presence was remarkable. Still, it cannot be said that these four contributed anything new to the internationalist movement; rather, their speeches betrayed a self-consciousness about being admitted into the august company of intellectual leaders from the West. Okakura had already published treatises on the distinctive qualities of Asian culture, but he nonetheless acknowledged that his and the other Japanese presence at the congress primarily meant that their country was now being recognized as a member of the community of civilized nations—not that this fact would affect the predominantly Western orientation of international affairs, including the internationalist movement.[29]

Likewise, the more than one hundred international organi-

zations that were represented at the Brussels Union des Associations Internationales were all European or North American.
While a few worldwide institutions, such as the Universal
Postal Union, had non-Western memberships, their headquarters and policy-making agencies were all centered in Europe or
the United States. Even the International Council of Women,
founded in the United States in 1888 as "a fellowship of women
of all races, nations, creeds, and classes," had little non-Western participation.[30] And when, in 1909, the International
Olympic Committee invited Japan's Kanō Jigorō, an educator
known for his ardént interest in establishing judo as an international sport, to join the elite group, he was the first (and for
many years the only) Asian to serve. (It was only one year earlier, at the 1908 Stockholm Olympics, that Japan had participated in the games for the first time, sending two athletes.)[31]
These examples show that cultural internationalism, despite its
stress on cross-cultural communication, was, at that time, not
yet a global undertaking.

Nevertheless, serious questions began to be raised about the
possible significance, for an international community still
dominated by the West, of the appearance of Japan (and by implication other non-Western countries) as a "civilized" power.
At the beginning of the Sino-Japanese War, for instance,
Uchimura Kanzō, a leading Christian theologian, asserted
that this war would be different from all wars fought among
Western powers because, unlike them, it was a righteous war in
which the Japanese asked, not for any territorial or monetary
prize, but only for an opportunity to take civilization to
neighboring countries.[32] Uchimura was soon disillusioned by
the way his countrymen, drunk with victory, began demand-
ing huge reparations and territorial concessions from China.

The war, he concluded sadly, had been no different from other wars fought for selfish ends. However, others continued to be interested in the role Japan could play in world affairs in which it would not blindly follow the lead of the Western powers but propose an alternative to the existing emphasis on armed might and war preparedness.

It was in such a context that the dichotomy of East and West entered the vocabulary of internationalism. As developed by Japanese writers such as Tokutomi Sohō, Japan's development as a "civilized" power signaled the emergence of the East on the world horizon. The East could either confront the West to challenge its power or cooperate with it to try to build a more harmonious world order. In Sohō's words, it was Japan's obligation to "introduce the civilizations of East and West to each other, harmonize the relationship between the yellow and white races, and coalesce the whole of humanity so as to reach the ultimate goal of justice."[33] Highly abstract as such thought was, it nevertheless exemplified Japanese thinking at the time, indicating a fascination with the self-conscious emergence of a non-Western, nonwhite "civilized" power. The international community would have to accommodate the fact and to alter its character from one of Euro-American hegemony to that of East-West cooperation and coexistence. What such cooperation would entail, however, was never quite clear, and even as the Japanese grappled with the best ways of conceptualizing the equation, they became uneasily aware that East and West might not, after all, be able to harmonize their interests and ideals, because they comprised different races.

The racial question in the history of internationalism is itself a fascinating phenomenon. International cooperation was a relatively straightforward proposition when it was conceptually limited to Western nations sharing historical, religious, and racial roots. Internationalism could be proposed as an alternative to excessive nationalism by appealing to aspects of the shared tradition—for instance, the Christian concept of charity or the Kantian notion of republicanism. What happens, however, if more than one race or more than one civilizational tradition is involved? Internationalism then would entail interracial, intercultural communication and cooperation. Would it not be far more difficult to develop communication and cooperation between peoples of diverse historical backgrounds than among those whose main division, at least in modern times, was the national boundaries?

One of the remarkable coincidences of history is the fact that internationalist movements were making rapid gains in the West at the very moment when prejudices against non-Western people were also becoming widespread. Racial prejudice, of course, had existed earlier, but at the end of the nineteenth century and the beginning of the twentieth, both internationalism and racism—to use crude, shorthand expressions—gained recognition and respectability in Europe and North America. Thus, while international organizations mushroomed, anti-Semitism revived in Europe, eugenics as a scientific investigation of hereditary traits so as to "perfect the race" was established as an academic discipline, anti-Chinese and anti-Japanese immigration movements gained strength in the United States, and brutal colonial wars were fought in Africa, the Pacific, and the Caribbean against nonwhite races.

It would be too simplistic to argue that these seemingly contradictory developments were aspects of the same phenomenon; namely, Western imperialism. Both internationalism and racism were products of Western power and influence and reflected the predominant position held by Europe and North America in world commerce, strategic balances, and cultural activities. It could even be said that imperialism (including its assumed superiority of the white over other races) was a form of internationalism: it brought different races and cultures together and established an international "community." Imperialism spread Western civilization to non-Western areas of the world and thus contributed to developing a global awareness. On the other hand, contemporary observers viewed imperialism as a factor pushing the powers to war. As Lord Salisbury, the British prime minister during the 1880s and the 1890s, noted, "You may roughly divide the nations of the world as the living and the dying . . . the living nations will gradually encroach on the territory of the dying and the seeds of conflict among civilised nations will speedily appear."[34] To the extent that internationalism and racism were derived from divergent assumptions—whereas internationalism, at least in theory, was an open-ended, inclusive proposition, capable of incorporating all nations and all peoples, racism by definition was exclusionary—their simultaneous appearance challenged Western thought. For the question arose as to whether non-Westerners could participate in, and contribute to, internationalist movements, which had hitherto been almost exclusively conceived and carried out by Europeans and North Americans.

Some in the West found such questions uncomfortable to contemplate and, when they did so, responded by asking even more disturbing questions. Could people outside Europe and North America really fraternize with Europeans and Americans without undermining the latter's civilization? While Westerners were busy fighting against one another or dreaming of peace, were not these other races rapidly catching up with them, with a view ultimately to challenging their supremacy? As François Coppé, the French poet, wrote at the time of the Boxer expedition, "Even if all Europe should agree to peace and disarmament, what about the enormous and mysterious China? . . . Should such a country of four hundred million produce a Moltke, then the world would, in one day, be turned upside down by a new barbarian invasion." There was no reason why China, and by implication other non-Western countries, could not transform themselves, following the example of "the little Japan." This was the Yellow Peril concept that was rapidly gaining currency in the West. As Coppé asked, what could the Europeans do in the face of such a development—Europeans who had been enjoying the delicious fruits of peace and had lost their energies, presumably because of the movements for peace and internationalism? In such an equation, the very internationalism that was making headway was giving rise to racial fears. Coppé's solution was obvious; it was time to stop dreaming dreams of universal brotherhood and wake up to the need to strengthen Europe. In an interesting twist of logic, he even called for a new internationalism—an international alliance "for defending our racial and religious brothers . . . for Christianity and civilization."[35]

Obviously, such a solution would not appeal to everyone, and there were those in Europe and North America who were willing to contemplate a new world order in which West and non-West cooperated. For instance, Ernest Fenollosa, the American art critic, used the analogy of marriage to visualize an eventual union of the two halves of humanity. They needed each other, he asserted, as they complemented their respective qualities. Henri Cordier, the French historian, spoke of "the new Mediterranean called the Pacific Ocean" and predicted an

increasingly important role to be played by Americans and
Asians (especially Chinese) in turning the ocean into the new
center of international affairs. Basil Chamberlain, the foremost
British student of Japanese history and literature at that time,
traveled back and forth between Japan and Europe to foster a
sense of cultural equivalence between the two, not the superiority of one over the other. He found equivalence, for instance, between the traditional Japanese theater and Wagner-
ian operas. In 1911, several British statesmen, scholars, and
religious leaders, concerned over interracial tensions, organized a "universal races congress" in London. The participants, from most European countries as well as the United
States, Haiti, Brazil, Turkey, Persia, China, Japan, and others,
met for eight days and listened to papers on topics ranging
from "Meaning of Race, Tribe, and Nation" and "The Problem of Race Equality" to "The Jewish Race" and "The Treatment of Dependent Peoples and Communities." Although a
notable beginning, the conference did little to elucidate the
relationship between racial diversity and internationalism.
(Only one out of the nearly forty papers presented dealt directly with the issue of cross-cultural contact.)[36] It is hard to
escape the conclusion that before World War I few in Europe
or North America developed a conception of global internationalism, embracing different races and peoples.

Asian writers, in the meantime, had somehow to hope that
the blatantly racist arguments they saw in the West did not represent the prevailing view and that ultimately internationalism
would be broadened enough to accommodate the whole of
humanity—otherwise, they would either have to counter this
formulation by developing their own definition of internationalism or abandon the effort and retreat to an exclusionary

stance comparable to that of some Western writers. At this time, all three approaches were pursued simultaneously, but none of them could be said to have added significantly to the vocabulary of internationalism.

The thinking of Nitobe Inazō, the foremost Japanese internationalist, provides a good example. He ardently identified his country's modern history with that of the Western powers, embracing the Spencerian historicist view of civilizational progress that affected all societies. At the same time, he was a firm advocate of cultural internationalism. His first book written in English, *The Intercourse between the United States and Japan,* published in 1891, may be taken as a plea for mutual understanding and communication between the two peoples. In his popular *Bushido: the Soul of Japan,* first published in English in the United States in 1898 and subsequently translated into many languages, he sought to equate the history of Japan with that of the European countries, arguing that *bushidō,* or the warrior ethic, was Japan's equivalent of Europe's medieval chivalry. The samurai, or the warrior, had the characteristics of Friedrich Nietzsche's "hero," he added. In finding such parallels with European history, Nitobe was not merely engaging in nationalistic propaganda. In the book he noted, for instance, that the philosophy of Wang Yang-ming, which had exerted a strong influence on Japanese thought, read like the New Testament or mystical writers like Isaac Pennington. Such an attempt at universalizing Asian thought was reflective of Nitobe's interest in persuading Europeans and North Americans to accept Asians as their equals, so that together they could contribute to a more just and peaceful world.

Underneath such optimism, however, lay an acute consciousness about racial issues. Nitobe himself had married an

American woman, but he knew that in many parts of the United States interracial marriages were prohibited by law. (Her father had never approved of the marriage.) And the immigration dispute between Japan and the United States could not but attract his attention.

Nitobe's response to the crisis was not to turn away from internationalism but to try to strengthen it through educational and cultural exchanges. During 1911–12 he was chosen as the first exchange lecturer to be sent from Japan to several U.S. universities under the auspices of the Carnegie Endowment for International Peace, established in 1910. (The Endowment was a good example of pre-1914 internationalism, and it is of considerable interest that its committee on "exchange and education" should have chosen as its first project the initiation of exchange professorships between the United States and Japan.)[37] Nitobe's message as he toured U.S. campuses was simple; time and again he reiterated his desire to transmit "the ideas of the West to the East, and of the East to the West." He attacked "dilettante ethnologists and amateur sociologists" for "the imagined abyss between the East and the West" and asserted that "it is the duty of every lover of humanity and of peace to be an interpreter, a go-between in the supposed clash of national interests and racial sentiments."[38]

Unfortunately for Nitobe, the "imagined" and "supposed" gaps between different races appeared to grow stronger than the internationalist forces. Asakawa Kan'ichi, a Japanese historian beginning his distinguished career teaching at Yale University, noted that no matter what he, or Nitobe, or others tried to do, American audiences seemed to have already developed preconceived ideas about Japan and U.S.-Japanese relations, at the same time assuming that the Japanese speakers

had come with certain prejudices as well. Under the circumstances, such efforts as Nitobe's lecture tour were destined to
be futile.[39] In such a situation, it was tempting to give up the
attempts at multiracial internationalism. For a scholar like
Asakawa, the best and the only way to bridge the gaps among
nations was through genuine scholarly endeavors; if respected
academics, rather than popular publicists like Nitobe, could
visit other countries and interact with their counterparts
there, as was being done among North American and European scholars, their influence, while less immediately apparent, would in the long run prove to be more effective. But
Asakawa despaired that there were few distinguished intellectuals in Japan who could undertake such a task in Western
countries.

In the meantime, some thinkers in Japan, China, and elsewhere sought to develop their own brand of internationalism,
regardless of what went on in the West. Some would follow
the lead of the Chinese philosopher, K'ang Yu-wei, who in the
1880s and the 1890s developed the idea of *ta t'ung* or "the
great unity" that would be the culminating stage in human
history. Although formulated in the context of Chinese history, *ta t'ung* envisaged a world without wars in which all people lived in harmony. K'ang Yu-wei based such optimism on
his reading of the Confucian classics as well as contemporary
international affairs and believed that, just as Confucius had
predicted the coming of the age of peace after China's "war-
ring states" had finished fighting one another, humanity
would ultimately overcome its warlike tendencies and unite in
establishing "one world." Like some Western internationalists,
he mentioned with approval modern improvements in communications and transportation technology, as well as interna-

tional agreements on postal rates and other matters; also like them, K'ang saw many "boundaries" dividing humanity: tribes, classes, races, families. But he believed these could gradually be overcome through adjustment and reform. For instance, different races would be amalgamated through "migration, mixed marriages, and diet," as summarized by K'ang's leading interpreter, Laurence G. Thompson.[40]

However influential in Chinese circles—and some of K'ang's ideas were published in book form in 1913—such optimistic thought gained few adherents elsewhere at this time. More appealing to Asians was pan-Asianism, the formulation summed up in Okakura Tenshin's assertion that "Asia is one." Okakura, the U.S.-educated art critic and literary figure, represented the views of those who imagined a unitary East as the counterpoint to the West. Not that he thought East and West were totally antagonistic to each other, but he believed the best way to bridge the gap between them was through the East's asserting its own identity as a civilization.

It was only a step from here to the concept of Asian solidarity opposed to Western power and influence, a view that gained currency at the turn of the century and grew influential in the aftermath of the Russo-Japanese War. Initially focused on China and Japan, the idea of Asian solidarity assumed an approximation, if not an identity, of interests on the part of these countries, set against the Western nations. This idea sought to counter the type of racialist thought exemplified by Coppé by coalescing all, or at least some, of the non-Western, nonwhite peoples of the world. There was frequent talk, from Egypt to India, from China to Japan, and even among black Americans in the South, of a race conflict in which the colored races would take on the dominant white race. (Hafiz Ibrahim, the Egyptian poet, referred to the Russo-Japanese War as a racial conflict and considered Japan's victory a great opportunity for bringing equal rights to all colored races. Likewise, Jawaharlal Nehru records that the war, which broke out when he was fourteen, "stirred up [his] enthusiasm" and encouraged him to consider fighting for "Asian freedom from the thralldom of Europe.")[41] Less extreme were ideas of Chinese-Japanese solidarity expressed, for instance, by Konoe Atsumaro and his circles of friends, in both countries, who organized a Society for People of the Same Letters in East Asia (Tōa Dōbun Kai), dedicated to the ideal of preserving the interests of China and Japan. The expression, "the same letters, the same race" (*t'ung-wen t'ung-chung* in Chinese; *dōbun dōshu* in Japanese) had been used by Li Hung-chang, the Chinese plenipotentiary, at the peace conference of 1895, which brought the Sino-Japanese War to a close, and was as familiar a concept in that part of the world as was Anglo-Saxonism elsewhere.

The stress on racial diversity, whether it took an extreme or a less extravagant form, was obviously counter to the ideal of internationalism. Pan-Asianism or Chinese-Japanese solidarity would envisage an Asia separate from the West, with its own philosophies and interests. Some of these ideas and movements could have developed into a new variety of internationalism, one in which regional and cultural identities would constitute an important foundation. But such a development lay in the future. For the time being, there was no attempt at redefining Western-centered internationalism through an accommodation with the increasingly self-conscious forces asserting racial and cultural identities, whether in the West or elsewhere. This was an age in which a British journalist could confidently assert that "the superior races [have] a mission . . . to rule the world," or when a well-known historian, also of Britain, could observe without a trace of self-consciousness, that "the desire to preserve racial purity is common to the higher nations."[42] Such self-confident views were incompatible with the aroused self-assertiveness on the part of non-European races. The Western internationalists, although undoubtedly having made very promising beginnings, had not yet fully comprehended the magnitude of the reality: the real world of racial and cultural diversity. In the meantime, even among "the higher races" of Europe, internationalist forces were becoming submerged once again under forces that were leading inexorably to the catastrophe of 1914.

The world of 1914 was still dominated by geopolitical realism; that is, the great powers' quest for military might, imperial dominion, and economic resources in which conflict, actual or potential, among nations was taken for granted. It was a world little removed from the one Rousseau had imagined when he wrote that "war is natural between the Powers" because any state "feels itself weak if there is another that is stronger."[43] Yet, at the same time, there had developed movements that refused to accept such an image of interstate relations and proposed alternative ways of conceptualizing international affairs. Some of the movements were internationalist in explicitly seeking to build institutions and mechanisms across national boundaries so that they would constitute the basis of a more stable world order. Cultural internationalism was a relative latecomer to the scene, but on the eve of World War I it had gained momentum, as could be seen in the mushrooming of organizations and conferences that brought artists, scientists, religious leaders, and many others together to develop an awareness of shared interests and perspectives.

Unfortunately, internationalism in general and cultural internationalism in particular proved woefully inadequate to prevent the booming of the "guns of August." Future internationalists, if they were to revive the movement, would have to consider more effective ways of bringing culture to power. In the meantime, pre-1914 cultural internationalism contained a serious flaw: having hardly gone beyond the perimeters of Western civilization, it tended to ignore the problem of cultural diversity, a problem that even then was impinging upon the movement through the vexing issue of interracial relations. This, too, was something postwar internationalists would have to confront if they were to make their efforts more appealing internationally.

CHAPTER TWO

The Origins of
Cultural Internationalism

Cultural internationalism came of age in the aftermath of
World War I. There was a real determination on the part
of its earlier advocates as well as new adherents to take specific
steps to promote the cause. In the years immediately following
the Paris peace conference, cultural internationalist organizations mushroomed, and during the 1920s the movement
flourished as it had never done before. Compared with its prewar variety, it was now not only much wider in scope but also
less elitist and less confined to Europe and North America.

Shortly before the European nations plunged into war in August 1914, betraying the hopes of internationalists that war
among civilized states was destined to become obsolete, Gustave Hervé, who had, only a few years earlier, published an ardent plea for internationalism, wrote an essay for *Guerre so-
ciale,* a socialist organ dedicated to war preparedness, warning
of the danger of German militarism. That a socialist internationalist like Hervé, who had ridiculed national subdivisions of
humanity, should now be writing for such a journal was reflective of the resurgent nationalism in the face of the July crisis. He argued that the Serbs and other Slavic populations in

the Balkans were justified in wanting to have "free national sovereignties of their destiny, grouping people of the same race in a national entity." Even though he was not advocating that France go to war to support Serbian nationalism, he enthusiastically embraced the war with Germany when it came. If the socialists could not save the peace, he wrote on August 1, then they had the duty to save the country from invasion. Although he was forty-three years old, he said, he would be the first to volunteer for military service. Hervé did try to reconcile his acceptance of war with his earlier denunciation of it in the name of internationalism by insisting, "We take up arms in order to establish, with the help of the German republic, a republic of the united states of Europe."[1]

Far less subtle, and much more shocking, was the transformation of Urbain Gohier's ideas. "We have sacrificed much for peace," he wrote shortly after the outbreak of the war, "but how can we impose peace on a nation . . . so full of hate and cupidity [Germany], except by war?" The erstwhile internationalist who had called for the lowering of national walls of separation to create a united states of Europe now became a champion of antiforeignism, urging the government to drive out foreigners from Paris and even to get rid of naturalized citizens. They were infesting the streets of the great city while "our own people are dying at the front," he wrote; such "an army of crime" should be sent to *"les camps de concentration,"* otherwise "our glory would be a farce, and our sacrifice an atrocious despair."[2]

Once the image of a peaceful world order that had sustained internationalism crumbled, the opposite vocabulary, ranging from patriotism and nationalism to antiforeignism and racism, returned with a fury to turn the whole of Europe into competitive fragments. The imagined international community of the prewar years was now replaced by a picture of the world in which national sovereignties appeared once again to be the only reality that mattered. There was little that could mediate between nationalism and internationalism, between war and peace. Richard Dehmel, the German poet who had tried to be "a good European" before the war, laying the groundwork for an all-embracing feeling of humanity, volunteered for military service as an act of penance; he wanted to share his people's fate and to be merged with them.[3] Another German writer, Sigmund Graff, observed that "the discovery of the Great War, the only discovery which made the war worthwhile for us, was the German human being [*der deutsche Mensch*]."[4]

The transformation of cultural elites into wartime patriots was a theme in George Bernard Shaw's play *Heartbreak House,* originally published in 1916 though not performed until after the war. The playwright satirized what he viewed as the unbridgeable gap between men and women of "culture" and those of "power." The former included artists, musicians, intellectuals, and all those whose primary preoccupation was with cultural pursuits and who had little understanding of anything else. The latter referred to politicians, businessmen, and others whose interest lay in the accumulation of wealth and power but who had little cultural sophistication. The two never interacted and remained ignorant of each other, and thus culture and power remained compartmentalized—until, Shaw noted in the play's preface (entitled "Culture and Power"), war came; then all of a sudden everyone was caught up in patriotic frenzy and outdid one another in the service of the country. He believed, however, that despite this wartime patriotism the gap between culture and power would remain.[5]

Shaw may have been too pessimistic. True, everything he said about the powerlessness of culture to confront the reality of power was all too evident during the war. At the same time, however, the European fratricide, which also came to involve such extra-European powers as the United States, Japan, and China, in time produced a powerful counterwave that prepared the ground for the renewal of internationalism after the war. Actually, the publication, during the war, of books like *International Government* by Leonard Woolf and *Mitteleuropa* by Friedrich Naumann (both mentioned in chapter 1) suggests that even in the heat of fanatical patriotism some continued to believe in certain long-term trends in modern history that would, despite temporary setbacks, inevitably usher in a more interdependent, cooperative world. That may have impressed wartime readers as too optimistic, but the longer the war lasted to the frustration of nationalists everywhere, the stronger grew the likelihood that internationalism would resurface as the key to reestablishing world order.

It is not surprising that, just as the coming of the war unleashed nationalistic emotions and submerged internationalist forces, its prolongation had the effect of once again forcing people to question the system of interstate relations founded on national sovereignties, identities, and interests. Whereas prewar internationalism was essentially an intellectual product, developed by people who had not experienced the total war of the kind now being waged, the internationalist movements that developed during the war and vastly expanded after its end were sustained by intimate personal experiences, whether at the trenches, at sea, or at the home front. "The aims of the war may be inspiring," wrote a German university student at the front, "but the means are the despicable and loathsome methods of mass murder." The war, another observed, "is the most horrible miscarriage of human vices and the treacherous, cruel assassin." As the fighting neared its end, a student noted, "The war that had started with such freshness of youth ends like a boring, stale, over-powered, and rouged actor who has outlived himself. Only death is victor. We shall all be damaged somehow, at least in what is called Weltanschauung."[6] A soldier in Ernest Johannsen's novel, *Four Privates: Their Last Days at the Western Front,* published in 1929, asks,

Will the death of these thousands of men mean more than a falling leaf that somehow floats down gently in a forest; do millions not count more than an ant? Is all mankind nothing but a trifle in the huge game of existence? Are they all only manure for the earth and nothing more? . . . And if in the last few minutes shortly before death your pains would suddenly stop and someone would come and say it had been 'God's inscrutable will' that had made you hang there with dangling intestines and scream for eight hours before you finally kicked off, you will perhaps, with the last of your strength (you are too weak to speak) spit into his face.[7]

What is striking about these depictions of the horrors of war is the universalizing of the particular experience; that is, the tendency to talk of humanity and human destiny in connection with the fates of individuals. It is as if the war had obliterated national distinctions and united soldiers of all countries through their shared suffering.

In the preceding chapter, I quoted from Leon Trotsky's remark in 1917 that the war had established a connection between "the fate of an individual and the fate of all mankind." That connection was important because it imagined a worldwide community consisting of individual humans no longer separated by the artificial barriers of sovereign states. That was what gave hope to those who struggled to reaffirm and strengthen internationalism in the wake of the calamitous war. For many European leaders, the submergence of internationalism, in particular the cultural internationalism that had seemed to have emerged so promisingly before the war, under excessive nationalism had been the most deplorable aspect of the conflict. Educated elites themselves had been guilty of this development, as they had embraced power politics and called on the masses to reject the cultural influences of enemy nations. Deeply embarrassed and ashamed of their wartime behavior, many erstwhile internationalists, as well as new converts, now vowed to dedicate themselves to resuscitating and expanding that movement as the only hope for a sane world order.

As if to reaffirm the spirit of cultural internationalism and to resume the tasks defined by the prewar internationalist leaders, in 1919 a group of intellectuals led by Romain Rolland issued a manifesto that would become famous, singling out cultural freedom and internationalism as the key to the postwar peace. As they said, European intellectuals had placed their science, their art, and their reason at the service of the egoistic interests of the states: they must never do so again; instead, they would now honor only one truth, "free, without frontiers, without limits, without prejudices of race or caste." To overcome narrow nationalisms and embrace a cosmopolitan identity, this was the task these cultural leaders put before themselves as they greeted the coming of the peace.[8]

For Rolland and his colleagues it was axiomatic that the postwar world order must have a solid foundation on cultural communication and exchange. As Paul Valéry noted, "a league of human intellects," not just an association of nations, was needed to establish a peaceful world. Henri Bergson agreed, asserting, "When the mentality of other nations was understood, the world would be much more ready to agree" on matters of war and peace.[9] To these voices, other prominent Europeans added theirs. Marie Curie, Albert Einstein, Fritz Haber, Ernst Troeltsch, Henri Pirenne, and many others were ardent advocates of postwar internationalism, especially of the cultural variety. Cultural internationalism did not, of course, arise as an entirely new movement from the ashes of the war, but it was elevated to a central position in postwar discussions of international affairs.

To be sure, the League of Nations was the most spectacular instance of postwar internationalism. It was the best example of political internationalism. As Thomas Knock has pointed out, the League owed its inspiration to currents of thought in wartime Britain and America that sought an alternative to traditional power politics.[10] The League was, in such a perspective, to be the embodiment of humanity's long search for an institution that would promote cooperation among nations to preserve the peace. Nothing like it had before been organized on a worldwide basis. This stress on institutionalization reflected the belief that good intentions were not enough to ensure a peaceful world order and that they must be translated into organizational form.

It is interesting that among contemporary observers there was widespread recognition that the laissez-faire mechanism was no longer operative in a complex modern society and that everywhere men and women were organizing themselves: they formed trade unions, political movements both right and left, business associations, neighborhood groups, women's federations. In an insightful book published in 1918, Mary Follett, a

U.S. political scientist, called for the construction of a "new state" on the principle of "group organization." Likewise, William Y. Elliott, a Harvard scholar, noted that, in order to survive, the democratic states would have to be rebuilt on the basis of "co-organism."[11] Follett and Elliott were typical voices of the age. The twentieth century, Follett asserted, "must find a new principle of association. Crowd philosophy, crowd government, crowd patriotism must go. . . . Group organization is to be the new method in politics, the basis of our future industrial system, the foundation of international order." The League of Nations, then, came into existence not as an isolated phenomenon but as an integral part of the post-war emphasis on organization. Its founders believed that, just as in the domestic context different interests and orientations of citizens must be reassembled through a network of organizations, the League would exemplify "the group consciousness rising from the national to the international unit."[12]

International was now more globally construed than before the war. From the beginning, it was assumed that not only would the two key extra-European nations, the United States and Japan, play pivotal roles in the world organization as permanent members of the Council (the other members being Britain, France, and Italy), but that scores of countries outside of Europe and North America would also be represented. Indeed, of the thirty-two original members of the League when it officially began its life in January 1920, only ten were from Europe. Eleven represented states from Central and South America, and nine came from other parts of the world. (The United States soon dropped out when the Senate refused to ratify the Versailles peace settlement.) The numbers alone indicated that the age of the great European powers, when their dealings with one another virtually defined the world order, was over. The international community was visibly more global, with obvious implications for internationalism.

Alongside political internationalism, economic (or liberal capitalist) internationalism, which had existed earlier, was also revived after the war and provided an important aspect of the imagined world community. Ernest E. Calkins, an American writer, was echoing a widely shared view when he wrote in 1928, "The work that religion, government, and war have failed in must be done by business. . . . Business has become the world's greatest benefactor." Henry Ford agreed, arguing that, in the postwar world, capital, technology, productivity, and efficiency, not armed force, would define national and international affairs. Because these resources and capabilities were most abundantly available in the United States, postwar economic internationalism was often synonymous with the idea that U.S. liberal capitalism would shape the world. As Reinhold Niebuhr wrote in 1932, after the onset of the Depression but still reflecting the prevailing perspectives of the 1920s, "We are living in an economic age, and the significant power is economic rather than military." The United States was "the first empire of the world to establish [its] sway without legions." In such a situation, "social and political relationships" throughout the world could be adjusted "by the use of economic force without recourse to the more dramatic display of military power."[13]

Economic internationalism clearly was a major influence in the postwar decade. Capitalists, businessmen, and industrialists contributed immeasurably to postwar economic recovery and development in Europe, Asia, and elsewhere. In effect, they envisaged a world of commercial interdependence, with the United States as the major provider of capital, technology, and goods, as an alternative to the geopolitical definition of international affairs that had seemingly become bankrupt.

The history of post–World War I internationalism, however, would be incomplete without the inclusion of an account of the cultural variety, which in many ways was a more novel force and pushed with even greater vigor than business internationalism. Precisely because cultural internationalism had been weaker than economic internationalism before the war, exponents of the former movement redoubled their efforts to place it at center stage. The postwar internationalists believed that what was really novel about their movement for peace was the stress on cultural, intellectual, and psychological underpinnings of the international order; that at bottom, peace and order must depend on a habit of mind on the part of individuals in all countries—a mindset that looked beyond security, legal, and even business issues and was willing to link national to world interests. As Follett wrote, "The old-fashioned hero went out to conquer his enemy; the modern hero goes out to disarm his enemy through creating a mutual understanding." Such understanding, she continued, could be promoted only if nations created "a group culture which shall be broader than the culture of one nation alone."[14]

As is evident in such statements, cultural internationalism was, at one level, an intellectual proposition. The cultural internationalists agreed that the key to peace lay in cross-national understanding, which in turn had to be built solidly upon active cooperation of cultural elites. Intellectual cooperation, the term that came to be used widely in the 1920s, was as important as cooperation in security, political, or economic issues. Intellectual cooperation committees sprang up in many countries, with links to the League's Committee on Intellectual Cooperation (discussed later in this chapter). Frank Heath, secretary of the British committee, explained that the existence in each country of "a small group of men and women . . . who have the means of influencing opinion in their own nation" was the best guarantee of international amity. "The realm to be conquered," he wrote, "is the Kingdom of Knowledge and Ideas and it can only be internationally organised through the agency of men and women of knowledge and ideas."[15] There is a direct link between such ideas and Rolland's declaration of intellectual freedom: intellectuals and cultural elites of all countries were envisaged as the new crusaders who would be willing to transcend parochial concerns and unite with one another to promote mutual understanding.

There was little new in the idea of cultural communication as such. Cosmopolitanism, postulating a "republic of letters," had long existed in the West side by side geopolitics. Europeans and North Americans had begun, before 1914, to establish organizations to further the movement. In the wake of World War I, however, there was not only greater self-consciousness about cultural cooperation as an instrument for peace, but its scope came to be broadened, to embrace other regions of the world—and therefore other civilizations and traditions. In part, this reflected the awareness that intra-Western internationalism was not enough; that just as the League of Nations included many non-Western members, postwar cosmopolitanism must become truly global.

This was far from being a simple phenomenon. For one thing, the war had brought into question the complacent assumption that the West represented the world; that what the "civilized" countries did among themselves defined the state of international relations, whether political, economic, or cultural. Now there grew not only loss of confidence on the part of Europeans—"Europe is sick, perhaps dying," wrote Anatole France—but also its opposite elsewhere, self-consciousness and assertiveness on the part of people in the Middle East, Asia, and elsewhere.[16] Of course, such self-consciousness had been in existence before the war, especially in the aftermath of the Russo-Japanese War. Now, however, Europeans themselves agreed that their material and spiritual superiority might be coming to an end. Some responded to this defensively, reaffirming the need to fortify the West against the expected onslaught on the part of the non-West. The continued vogue of eugenics, as exemplified by the popularity of books like Madison Grant's *The Passing of the Great Race* (1916), was an indication of this. Many argued that "the threat to white prestige," as a French theologian put it, could be alleviated only when "the great culture and rich legacy" of Europeans were shared with other people.[17] Others focused on building a peaceful European community in which all, former allies and enemies alike, would pool their energies and resources for the good of the whole region. (It is interesting to note that Richard N. Coudenhove-Kalergi, one of the best-known exponents of this movement and the founder of the Paneuropa-Union, was the son of an Austrian diplomat and a Japanese mother.) Still others looked outward, in the direction of the United States or of the Soviet Union, as the possible solution to Europe's ills, with which the European countries alone did not seem capable of coping.

Among such a galaxy of responses, one notable development was a new cosmopolitanism—an eagerness to embrace the whole of humanity, or at least many more countries and peoples than had been envisaged in earlier, Western-oriented conceptions of international order. This sensitivity to cultural diversity may be seen, for instance, in the League's adoption of a rule, in 1922, that the six nonpermanent members of its Council were to be selected "with due consideration for the main geographical divisions of the world, the great ethnical groups, the different religious traditions, the various types of civilization and the chief sources of wealth." This decision was arrived at after the Chinese delegate had made a plea for what later would be called affirmative action—the inclusion on the Council of at least one representative from "Asia and the remaining [non-Western] parts of the world."[18]

Such a situation was highly favorable for the broadening of cultural internationalism. Rather than reverting to the prewar pattern of Eurocentric agendas, postwar internationalism could embrace cultural and intellectual communication among diverse cultures and philosophies. As often as not, the agents of such communication would be Asians and South Americans. This globalization of internationalism was one of the most striking developments of the postwar years.

At one of the first meetings of the League of Nations, the Indian delegate called for "internationalization of ideas and conditions," and a Haitian scholar argued that all countries ought to undertake school reforms in order to promote the idea of peace. It is remarkable not only that these delegates taking an early initiative in broadening the scope of cultural internationalism were non-Westerners but that they were being eagerly listened to. When, in March 1922, the League invited fifty-eight prominent intellectuals to discuss the founding of a committee on intellectual cooperation, it made sure that they would come not only from Europe—including Germany, although Germany had not yet been allowed to join the world organization—but also from the United States, Latin America, and Asia.[19] (The fifty-eight included representatives from Japan, India, Brazil, Uruguay, Argentina, Paraguay, Colombia, the United States, and Europe.) Their deliberations resulted in the establishment in Geneva of the International Committee on Intellectual Cooperation. It was to be a permanent part of the world organization. A sister grouping, the International Institute for Intellectual Cooperation, was organized in Paris in 1926 with initial financial support from the French government, supplemented by contributions from many countries in Europe, Latin America, the Middle East, and Asia. Tied to these institutions in Geneva and Paris were national committees on intellectual cooperation, created in as many as thirty-four countries by the end of the 1920s.

In Britain, for example, in 1928 Foreign Secretary Austen Chamberlain asked the classicist Gilbert Murray to gather together representatives of "the learned societies and organisations which represent intellectual life in this country." Murray invited such individuals as Frederick Kenyon, director of the British Museum, the historian G. P. Gooch, and the poet (later president of the Royal Academy) J. W. MacKail to constitute the national committee.[20] The British committee under Murray, as well as its unofficial spokesman, the classical historian Alfred Zimmern, worked heroically with a token subsidy of only £300 annually from the Foreign Office, with the members often paying out of their own pockets for travel, postage, and other expenses.

In Japan, to cite another example, a League of Nations association founded immediately after the war, in 1926 established a subcommittee on intellectual exchange.[21] Nitobe

Inazō, mentioned in the preceding chapter as Japan's foremost internationalist before the war, was for several years both undersecretary-general of the League (specifically charged with intellectual cooperation) and chairman of the Japanese delegation to the Committee on Intellectual Cooperation in Geneva. The appointment of a Japanese scholar as undersecretary-general indicated that, from its inception, the League's work was envisaged as intellectual as well as political, and that non-Western participation in intellectual activities would be very important.

Even more striking was U.S. participation in the work of this committee. Because the United States did not join the League, intellectual cooperation was promoted much more extensively outside, rather than through, the world organization, but even so, private individuals such as Raymond Fosdick of the Rockefeller Foundation and James Shotwell, the Columbia University historian, were extremely active throughout the interwar years. The Rockefeller Foundation granted Shotwell small sums of money so that he could establish a U.S. committee on intellectual cooperation on the campus of Columbia University. Shotwell and his executive secretary (he had no other support staff) carried out voluminous correspondence with both Americans and non-Americans who shared their commitment and interests.[22] Though a small-scale operation, the committee laid the groundwork for what was later to develop into official programs of cultural exchange.

The idea of intellectual communication was unabashedly elitist. Those involved envisaged that the intellectual and cultural elites would befriend one another to establish a cross-national community of learned individuals. They strongly believed this was an important enterprise, especially in view of the failure of the cultural elites during the war to prevent chauvinistic excesses. Moreover, it was easier to promote intellectual and cultural cooperation with elites in non-Western countries than with the masses who, it must be admitted, remained largely untouched by the movement. Non-Western thinkers and artists, in any event, were comfortable fraternizing with their European and North American counterparts, and together they developed a sense of community, a cosmopolitan community that did not recognize artificial boundaries but was committed to broadening what later would be called "borderlands," a cultural space that belonged to no particular country but where people and cultural products of different societies would create their own identities and agendas.[23]

The idea that the world would, by cementing ties among cultural elites, come a step closer to the ideal of internationalism was put into practice in many ways. The League of Nations sponsored high-level conferences and exchanges of open letters among the intellectual leaders of the time. The most famous example of such letters was the much publicized correspondence on war and peace undertaken in 1932 by Albert Einstein and Sigmund Freud. Intellectuals not only from the West but also from the Middle East and Asia came together for symposia on topics ranging from "The future of letters" to "Goethe."

Activities in cultural cooperation outside the League framework were equally varied and impressive. New international organizations were added to the hundreds that had existed before the war. These ranged across many fields and subjects, from contemporary music to museum management, and international studies to journalism. Whereas before the war most international organizations had been in the fields of medicine, the sciences, mathematics, or practical affairs such as the regulation of postal and telegraphic rates, now every cultural activity was eager to internationalize itself. For instance, "the first international conference on popular arts" was held in Prague in 1928, and the first meeting of "the international concert federation" was organized in Budapest in 1929. (That new states like Czechoslovakia and Hungary should have hosted these gatherings is itself interesting, indicating that postwar cultural internationalism appealed to many countries outside the great powers.) The president of the concert federation, Count San Martino, reflected the prevailing spirit behind such undertakings when he stated that his organization sought to "find an element of international solidarity in the universality of artistic ideals."[24]

In the meantime, the field of international relations was developing. Scholars from various countries who were "engaged in the study of political, economic, social, and historical problems from an international standpoint" met in Berlin in 1928, and again in Copenhagen in 1931. It was in the 1920s that universities in the United States, Britain, and other countries began offering graduate programs in international relations. At the University of Chicago, a leading center of this endeavor, Quincy Wright, one of the foremost U.S. internationalists of the day, led a group of historians, political scientists, sociologists, economists, and others in a multiyear project to study the causes of wars. The idea was to develop a science of international relations through cross-disciplinary cooperation—a typical intellectual undertaking of the postwar years. In 1919, the *Journal of Race Development,* started at Clark University in 1910, changed its title to the *Journal of International Relations* and began publishing articles dealing with international, in particular Asian and Latin American, affairs. (Its board of editors included scholars from the United States, Korea, India, and the Philippines.)[25] In Geneva, in 1927, two scholars, William Rappard and Paul Mantoux, founded a new graduate institute of international studies to provide scholarly underpinnings for the League's activities in promoting international cooperation.

The development of this subfield in these countries coincided with the initiation of serious scholarly studies of contemporary non-Western societies. Given the globalization of intellectual activities, it was no accident that in the United States and Europe serious academic programs should have been initiated to train specialists in contemporary non-Western societies. The Social Science Research Council and the American Council of Learned Societies (ACLS), both established after World War I, sponsored programs at a number of U.S. academic institutions in what would later be called "area studies." (It is interesting to note that the ACLS was initially established in order to represent twelve scholarly organizations, including the American Historical Association and the Modern Language Association of America, in the Union Académique Internationale, which itself was another excellent example of postwar internationalism.)[26] Europe was still ahead in fields like the so-called Oriental studies (the study of ancient Middle Eastern civilizations) and Sinology (the study of Chinese civilization), and young Americans were sent to London, Paris, Leiden, and elsewhere to develop their skills. Given the parallel development of area studies and international relations as scholarly fields, it is not surprising that these U.S. students (for example, John King Fairbank and Edwin O.

Reischauer, to cite only the best-known) should have become interested in combining the two fields and developed expertise in Western relations with non-Western countries.

These were essentially elite-oriented activities. One major characteristic of postwar internationalism, however, was the recognition from the very beginning that cultural internationalism must also be promoted among the mass of people in all countries. This, too, was a reflection of the awareness that the war had brought huge numbers of people from different countries together, and that their aroused emotions had done much damage to stable international relations. If peace were to endure, therefore, it was critically important to prepare ordinary people throughout the world for less parochial, more global outlooks. Although most people outside of Europe and North America had not been directly involved in the fighting, their views were just as important as those of people in the West because industrialization was slowly coming their way. Popular nationalism in non-Western societies, as exemplified by the May Fourth (1919) and the May Thirtieth (1925) movements in China, was a relatively new phenomenon. For the first time, any definition of internationalism would have to accommodate these developments. As William Y. Elliott noted, Asians were becoming more and more nationalistic at the very moment that the West was turning internationalist.[27] It was imperative, then, to promote a more global and more mass-based form of internationalism.

It was widely recognized that the masses, whether in Europe, North America, or elsewhere, were coming under the pervasive influence of modern technology, above all the radio, the cinema, and the telephone. Although these innovations had all been developed prior to World War I, their use had been limited mostly to urban populations in industrialized countries; notably, the United States. Now for the first time they were being far more extensively disseminated. These inventions, plus the automobile, seemed to symbolize the coming of a new age of mass communication and popularization of cultural pursuits. Robert Park, a University of Chicago sociologist, noted, "The forces which have brought about the existing interpenetration of peoples are so vast and irresistible that the resulting changes assume the character of a cosmic process."[28]

A key issue facing postwar internationalism, therefore, was whether these agents of mass culture could be turned into instruments of peace and understanding across national boundaries. That they could be utilized in the traditional way, to enhance one country's power and influence at the expense of other nations, could be seen in the movie industry, where there was as much nationalistic rivalry as before the war. The United States, Britain, France, Germany, and others vied with one another in marketing their products. Hollywood was determined to put an end to the European domination that had characterized the distribution of movies before the war and undertook an aggressive export drive. European officials and filmmakers, thus put on the defensive, struggled desperately to stem the tide, ultimately to no avail.[29] Most nations established regulations to govern the content as well as the distribution of movies in their effort to control the influx of foreign productions.

Such nationalistic tendencies threatened to undermine cultural internationalism, and serious efforts were made to establish frameworks to enable cross-national cooperation in employing the cinema for internationalist purposes. The best example of this came in 1928 with the founding of the International Educational Cinematographic Institute in Rome through the auspices of the League of Nations. That the headquarters of this institute was placed in Italy should be taken less as evidence of the fascist regime's success in a propaganda offensive than as a reflection of the prevailing atmosphere of the age; even such a regime found the prospect of being able to support the ideal of cultural internationalism to be irresistible. In any event, this organization proved to be, until Italy withdrew from the League in 1938, one of the most successful interwar experiments in cultural cooperation. The institute served as a clearinghouse of information on educational movies and worked hard to make it possible for such movies to be imported to recipient countries free of customs duties. The institute would issue a certificate for a movie that it, and the national committee on intellectual cooperation of the country where it was made, defined as educational cinema; the film would then enter other countries duty-free.[30] In 1929, to cite a related example, an international congress of "independent cinemas" was held in Switzerland to bring together representatives of smaller movie houses interested in showing foreign films. As cinema clubs mushroomed in a number of countries, they organized an international federation to facilitate the exchange of information.

Interwar internationalists were similarly extremely interested in the possibilities for cultural communication presented by the spread of radio transmitters throughout the world. In 1921, representatives from companies based in the United States, Britain, France, and Germany met in Paris to set up a joint system for South American radio broadcasting.[31] At the League, efforts were made to ensure that broadcasting in various countries would aim at promoting international understanding rather than nationalistic propaganda. It was much easier to aspire to such a goal than to realize it: there was no international agency to exercise any kind of censorship to ensure such an outcome, and radio programming was left in the hands of national and local authorities. Nevertheless, the internationalists understood that because of the very power of the new mass medium, it was extremely desirable to establish a system of cooperation about the content of broadcasting. Several national groups discussed the possibility of drafting an international agreement that would prohibit provocative programs inciting war and hatred and encourage those that spread better knowledge of "the civilization and the conditions of life of other peoples."[32] It proved difficult to obtain such an agreement among nations, but it is significant that the drafters continued to work on the project well into the 1930s.

It was widely recognized that ultimately internationalism must be built upon the education of more cosmopolitan, less narrowly nationalistic, individuals in all countries. The concern with educational cinema and with constructive broadcasting revealed that, although cultural internationalism was most visibly promoted at the elite level, the elites themselves were aware of the danger of confining their efforts only to individuals like themselves. Deeply fascinated by the spread of popular culture and concerned with mass nationalism, the internationalists believed that now, more than ever, education, the right kind of education at all levels, was of critical importance. Although each country had its own system for educating its youth, and it would therefore be next to impossible to internationalize national educational standards, there was a genuine interest among internationalists to do something in this sphere. They were particularly eager to promote two activities: the exchange of college and precollegiate students and teachers, and the revision of school textbooks. Neither objective went very far in the interwar years, but the fact that serious attempts were made in these directions fits into the overall phenomenon of cultural internationalism during this period and marks the 1920s as a distinctive phase in the history of internationalism.

The League of Nations was convinced that the exchange of teachers among nations "would have a very great effect on the promotion of international understanding upon which, in the long run, the peace of the world depends." In Geneva, the League held summer schools that were attended by students from all over the world, but much initiative in this direction was left to each country's committee on intellectual cooperation and other agencies. For instance, a modest program for exchanging schoolteachers began in the late 1920s among the United States, Britain, France, and Germany. In higher education, the same decade was particularly notable for increases in the number of student exchanges. Here, other governments emulated the U.S. example of hosting Chinese students through the Boxer indemnity funds, begun in 1908 as probably the only government-sponsored program of its kind at the time. Now Britain and Estonia, for instance, negotiated an agreement whereby part of the money the latter remitted to London annually to pay back wartime loans was earmarked for sending Estonian students to the United Kingdom. Britain also began using the Boxer indemnity funds for promoting student and worker exchanges with China.[33] In 1919 several foundations in the United States cooperated in establishing the Institute of International Education, an organization designed for coordinating student and teacher exchange programs. In Europe, in the meantime—following the signing, in 1925, of treaties between Germany and its European neighbors at Locarno—"the spirit of Locarno" was exemplified in the coming together of French and German students in annual gatherings, the first of which took place in Davos, Switzerland, in 1928.[34]

In Japan, as early as 1919 the Diet began discussing the value of bringing Chinese students to the country, and four years later the Foreign Ministry established a Chinese cultural affairs bureau, the only governmental agency of the kind anywhere in the 1920s.[35] Although there had been Chinese students in Japan—as many as eight thousand of them were there in 1905—they had not been part of a government-sponsored program of student exchange. In 1924, Chinese and Japanese officials signed an agreement whereby "cultural programs" would be promoted between the two countries, most notably the offer of scholarships to Chinese students in Japan (up to 320 students a year). The student program, like its counterparts elsewhere, was to be financed mostly through unused portions of the Boxer funds.[36] In 1927, the bureau, now renamed the office of cultural affairs, expanded its activities to promote exchanges with other Asian countries as well as Europe and the Americas. It was around this time that a new First School of Foreign Languages was established in Tokyo for the teaching of foreign languages (including Chinese, and also the Japanese language to Chinese students). European languages had been taught in Japan since the midnineteenth century, but the vogue for Chinese language study was a relatively new phenomenon and expressed a serious interest in establishing intellectual ties anew with the neighboring country.[37] Virtually for the first time in modern history, China and Japan came to define their relations in cultural, in addition to political and economic, terms. Language textbooks in both countries began incorporating contemporary literary works, and some of the books' authors visited one another.

The publication of new textbooks in Chinese and Japanese was in a way part of a larger phenomenon: after the war, many in Europe and elsewhere came to consider the rewriting of school textbooks particularly important as a means for promoting cross-national understanding. Too often, it was said, textbooks in history, geography, civics, and related subjects had fostered a narrowly nationalistic outlook and made it impossible for students to embrace any sort of internationalism. To remedy the situation, in 1926 a group of French and German teachers founded an "international institute for textbook revision in the cause of peace," with headquarters in Amsterdam.[38] In the following year, the League's Committee on Intellectual Cooperation called for "elimination from school textbooks of passages prejudicial to mutual understanding." It was reported that already nineteen countries had taken steps to revise school textbooks in order "to adapt them to ideas of international relations."[39]

The historian Eileen Power, who spearheaded the movement for the rewriting of history textbooks in Britain, noted that "inaccurate passages in school text books [are] likely to lead to bad international feelings." Textbooks, she asserted, must be judged "from the point of view of their accuracy and fairness in the treatment of international affairs."[40] How should this be done? Here again the national committees on intellectual cooperation provided the institutional framework. They corresponded with one another through the Paris Institute for Intellectual Cooperation, and each of them organized a network of textbook writers in their own country and sought to elicit specific suggestions for textbook revision. (In Britain, for instance, G. P. Gooch was made chairman of a committee to examine elementary and secondary school textbooks.) The institute created "a committee of experts for the revision of school textbooks," and one of the committee's reports stressed the importance of the teaching of history "in connection with the training of rising generations in a spirit of peace and good-will."[41] Such lofty language did not lead to the actual production of revised textbooks, except in a few instances. In most countries, governmental authorities, central or local, controlled textbook writing and distribution, and they were reluctant to yield this control to an international body, or even to a national committee oriented toward internationalism. In non-Western countries that were in the midst of nation-building efforts, moreover, nationalistic texts on history, geography, and civics were considered essential for creating a modern citizenry. Nevertheless, the idea of promoting international communication through textbooks that were less chauvinistic would not completely disappear, even during the 1930s, and it was to regain its influence after World War II.

An interesting related phenomenon in the educational scene between the wars was the vigorous promotion of Esperanto as a universal language. Although its founding spirit, Zamenhof, had died during the war, after 1919 Esperanto aroused much enthusiasm as a symbol of international communication. In December 1920, for instance, a resolution was introduced to the League of Nations assembly stating that the world organization, "well aware of the language difficulties that prevent a direct intercourse between the peoples," hoped that Esperanto would be taught throughout the world "so that the children of all countries may know at least two languages, their mother tongue [and Esperanto], an easy means of international communication."[42] Within two years, delegates from Brazil, Belgium, Chile, China, Colombia, Czechoslovakia, Haiti, India, Italy, Japan, Peru, Poland, and South Africa brought resolutions to the League, suggesting that the latter recommend the universal teaching of Esperanto in schools as an auxiliary international language.[43]

At the 1921 Esperanto congress in Prague, two hundred manual workers were present. They argued that "while the rich and the cultured enjoyed belles lettres and scientific treatises in the original, the poor and humble made of Esperanto a lingua franca for their exchange of views."[44] The Esperanto movement thus fitted into the growing popularization of cultural internationalism in the 1920s. Another trend, its globalization, could be seen in the gathering of Esperantists at their twenty-second congress, held at Oxford in August 1930, in which some 1,100 delegates from thirty countries participated. Like similar endeavors, the Esperanto movement never achieved the result it aspired to, but nevertheless it fitted into the overall cultural internationalist agendas of the 1920s. (An interesting example is Vasilii Eroshenko, a blind Russian poet and novelist who had studied Esperanto in Japan in 1914, got into trouble with the authorities because of his political activities, went to China to spread the movement after the war, and served as an intermediary between Chinese and Japanese linguistic internationalists.)

To these expressions of cultural internationalism after World War I, numerous other examples may be added. Journalists from various countries came together to promote better communication; as early as in 1920, more than one hundred newspaper and radio personnel from Latin America held a congress in Washington. Foreign tourism was given new meaning "as a means of international education," as was pointed out at a gathering of interuniversity student societies held in London in 1929.[45]

Statistics on foreign traveling are hard to come by, but the number of passports issued gives some indication of the trend. In the United States, for instance, approximately 203,000 passports were issued in 1930, an eightfold increase from 24,000 passports in 1910. This meant that, whereas one U.S. citizen in every 5,000 obtained a passport just before the war, the ratio narrowed to one out of 600 twenty years later. Not all these would have been for foreign travel, but it may safely be assumed that the increase could not have occurred without the growing popularity of tourism. (It is estimated that whereas only 2,000 to 5,000 U.S. tourists visited Japan during 1900–15, the number jumped to more than 55,000 for the decade 1920–30.)[46] Some travelers went abroad for only a few days, whereas others spent months circling the globe. Many stayed overseas for years. A clear link between foreign tourism/residence and internationalism can be seen in the example of U.S. women living in Paris who published a journal, *The Bulletin of the American Women's Club of Paris,* and declared, "As a Club in a foreign land, perhaps our most important work is in disseminating a spirit of friendliness between different nations. . . . In bringing foreigners together, we can be real factors for mutual understanding."[47]

Other natural venues for the practice of cultural internationalism that should be noted are museums and art galleries. This had not always been the case: some museum curators had been among the foremost advocates of eugenics and even of racism. But the postwar emphasis on cross-cultural communication and understanding brought about movements for using art exhibitions and similar displays to promote that goal. Typical was a Japanese exhibit in 1929 at the Detroit Institute of Art that, according to the Japanese ambassador commemorating the occasion, demonstrated the country's commitment to furthering "cultural interchange" as one way to contribute to "cultural and intellectual" understanding between Japan and the United States.[48] In New York, in the meantime, the Roerich Museum, which opened in 1923 with the core holding of more than three hundred paintings by Nicholas Roerich, explicitly aimed at "international unification through art." A Friends of Roerich Museum organization was established in the United States, France, Argentina, Chile, Peru, Uruguay, Yugoslavia, and Sweden to promote the idea of "an International Peace Pact which would protect all treasures of art and science through an International Flag."[49]

The Institute of Pacific Relations (IPR) was one of the most influential expressions of postwar internationalism. Established in Honolulu in 1925 and later moved to New York, the IPR brought together scholars, journalists, businessmen, and many others from the United States, Europe, and Asia for an exchange of views on Asian and Pacific issues. It held a general meeting every two years (in Honolulu in 1925 and 1927, Kyoto in 1929) to consider topics ranging from Japanese policy in China to Asian immigration (or nonimmigration) into the United States. This matter of immigration elicited considerable interest on the part of internationalists everywhere; they viewed the restrictive U.S. immigration policy (in particular the 1924 law excluding Orientals) as contrary to the spirit of postwar internationalism. Japan's foremost internationalist, Nitobe, was so enraged that he vowed never to visit the United States again until the law was repealed. Nationalistic feelings were aroused in Japan, which in turned fueled similar responses in the United States.

Among most internationalists, however, the typical reaction was to try to discuss points of agreement and disagreement so as to find areas for mutual accommodation. As discussed at Institute of Pacific Relations meetings and elsewhere, internationalist-oriented Americans and Japanese sought to promote a solution thereby Asians would be given a quota of annual immigration into the United States. However low the quota might be—it would have to be low, because the 1924 law specified that the annual quotas of immigrants reflect the U.S. national census of 1890—it would be far better than total prohibition, which was a clear case of racial discrimination. Little headway was made in this direction before the 1930s, but the episode suggests how willing and interested the internationalists were to tackle even the thorniest of issues in order to bring closer the fulfillment of their dream of an interdependent, cooperative world order.[50]

Not that every immigrant was a "cultural internationalist," any more than that every tourist, every exchange student, or every visitor to an art museum was. But cultural internationalism as a movement was fostered by the interpenetration of individuals from different lands, as some of them shared lives, ideas, and dreams together. Of course, others of them might, and did, react negatively to this experience, confirming their own parochialism. Cultural nationalists did not disappear, and in some instances they led movements to combat cosmopolitan influences. The United States provides a good example of this complex phenomenon. Postwar internationalism would not have been possible without U.S. economic, technological, and cultural influences, and in some instances it was even synonymous with them; yet nationalism was a notable feature of U.S. society and culture in the 1920s, as can be seen, for instance, in the carved stone monuments on Mount Rushmore—the decade's most visible contribution to the American memory—or in the findings in *Middletown,* a sociological study of Muncie, Indiana, undertaken by Robert and Helen Lynd, suggesting that nationalistic themes were stressed in the local educational system. The president of the board of education told the investigators, "We need to teach American children about American heroes and American ideals."[51] It seems hardly necessary to cite additional instances of extreme nationalism, bordering on xenophobia—the Red Scare, the Ku Klux Klan's activities in the North as well as in the South, the Sacco-Vanzetti trial—to realize the enormous obstacles faced by internationalists even in the United States.

At the same time, it is possible to view these nationalistic or xenophobic phenomena as a last-ditch reaction against what was perceived to be larger forces: the forces linking parts of the world closer together. Even in Muncie, the Lynds noted that "inventions imported from without—automobiles, motion pictures, and radio"—were connecting the community to the outside world, and that the city leaders' stress on nationalism was in some ways an attempt to retain a sense of solidarity and homogeneity in a period of profound transformation. It was only a step from here to the proposition that the best way to reaffirm American self-definition was not to eject alien elements or to eschew foreign contact but to stand for a new vision of the world in which American values and ways of life would spread to other lands. American civilization would be reinforced through its dissemination to the rest of the world. At least some commentators believed that that was the new mission of the United States: not to remain comfortable with its own traditions but to try to universalize them. Horace Kallen, one of the strongest critics of xenophobic nationalism, expressed the hope, in his influential book *Culture and Democracy*, that "Americanism as a social ideal could be identified with the ideal of culture, the culture of diversity and optimism. To be a citizen of the United States would then be the same in value as being a citizen of the world."[52]

Such a vision of culture made a significant contribution to the vocabulary of internationalism, and was indeed congruous with the philosophy of cultural internationalism being developed in Europe and elsewhere. The proposition that peace depended on the diffusion of culture gave a fresh perspective on international affairs. It was particularly appealing to U.S. internationalists because their government eschewed political involvement in world affairs. One of the most interesting commentators on this theme was the sociologist Robert Park. Writing in 1926 on cultural diffusion and race relations, he paid particular attention to the cinema, which, he said, "may be regarded as the symbol of a new dimension of our international and racial relations which is neither economic nor political, but cultural." The spread of the cinema as well as the popularity of the radio were affecting "men's minds and . . . their ultimate personal experiences." Motion pictures had "brought the ends of the earth into an intimacy unimaginable a few years ago." This intimacy, which was also fostered by the radio and the rapidly increasing literacy in all parts of the globe, was "steadily bringing all the peoples of the earth measurably within the limits of a common culture and a common historical life" so that the entire world was becoming a "melting pot."

The implications of such a development for international affairs were easy to see. Traditionally, Park wrote, wars had been fought to "establish and extend law and order in regions where it did not previously exist"; but by the same token war would become less necessary as the whole world came under a political and moral order thanks to cultural diffusion. Even though Park recognized that national and racial consciousness had not disappeared and in some instances had even intensified after the war, he interpreted this as evidence that there had come to exist "an international society and an international political order." Because cultural internationalization was proceeding rapidly, forces opposed to it would stress national and racial distinctiveness. But he was convinced that this, in particular the type of racial hostility as exemplified by the Asian exclusion law in the United States, was but a temporary phenomenon and would eventually give way to the far more potent force of internationalization. For the melting pot was no longer just the United States, but the entire world. The United States and the world were becoming closely integrated. That was why, in Park's words, "today is the most romantic period in the history of the whole world; not even the period of the discovery of America has influenced man's imagination more."[53]

Here cultural internationalism was clearly perceived as a mass phenomenon. Park saw the emergence of a new world community in which different parts of the globe were experiencing a common culture and narrowing moral and social distances between them. Because the United States was the center of the developing popular culture, the perceived new internationalism was virtually interchangeable with cultural Americanization. But it was not seen as a parochial phenomenon or as imperialism by other means. As Paul Johnson has noted, the 1920s saw the dialectical interplay of forces for universalism (what he calls "civilization") and for parochialism ("culture") throughout the world.[54] The terminology is confusing, but in the context of our discussion he is pointing to the same phenomenon as Park and many others. To borrow from the vocabulary of the 1990s, American culture was becoming "de-centered"; that is, it was spreading to other parts of the world and was no longer just "American."

Of course, in the domestic context, culture was being "produced," not automatically but through the medium of forces that were eager to reestablish some sort of order in a society that had gone through the turmoil of wartime mobilization and postwar readjustment. That these forces—forces of "normalcy"—were fundamentally business-oriented, stressing themes like prosperity, productivity, and efficiency, is clear. But these themes were easily exportable, as were cars, movies, and telephones. At the mass level, therefore, the more elitist notion of intellectual communication and cooperation was being amply reinforced through the agency of cultural Americanization. In this sense, the cultural internationalism of the 1920s may be said to have carried a step farther the earlier teleological conception of international relations, exemplified by Herbert Spencer, Leonard Woolf, and other internationalists, that the world was tending toward a more interdependent, less contentious community of peoples.

The picture becomes complicated because at that time there was another teleological view of history emanating from the new center of socialist internationalism, the Soviet Union.

As seen in the preceding chapter, the Second International had been a major agency promoting the idea of cross-national worker solidarity. But the movement collapsed as soon as war came in 1914. Five years later, after the founding of the Bolshevik regime in Russia, the Third International, or the Communist International as it came to be better known, was founded. Although nominally a successor to the failed Second International, the Comintern was more centrally controlled, and in time, especially after 1927 when Josef Stalin emerged as the successor to V. I. Lenin, it became more an instrument for the Soviet state than a force for proletarian internationalism. At the same time, the Soviet Union and the Comintern did make a contribution to enriching the vocabulary, and widening the scope, of cultural internationalism.

For example, the Comintern sponsored a number of international congresses, inviting writers and other cultural leaders from many countries to Moscow for an exchange of ideas. Obviously, these congresses were designed to enhance the prestige of the Soviet state, but this alone does not diminish their importance, because they added to similar activities being undertaken by bourgeois nations and served to increase opportunities for the world's intellectuals to mingle with one another. Moscow was also active in organizing youth conferences that tried to promote a worldwide movement against bourgeois civilization; at the same time, however, the Soviet leaders were not averse to cultural exchange as such, even with countries that did not recognize the new regime. The best example was the 1927 visit of jazz musicians from the United States.[55] Of course, they were not just anybody: by inviting a group of black musicians and lionizing them, the Soviet Union was transmitting a message about its stance on race equality. But at least until the late 1920s, when the First Five-Year Plan began and the Stalinist regime became more and more inward looking, the Soviet masses were encouraged to embrace these and other foreign visitors as brothers in pursuit of similar objectives.

The Comintern in the meantime sought to influence foreign opinions of the Soviet state through open propaganda as well as clandestine activities. While the bulk of these activities do not belong in the history of postwar internationalism, one should recognize that Comintern propaganda had the effect of spreading Marxism and Leninism abroad, especially among intellectuals, young and old. Comintern agents as well as directives emanating from Moscow had an enormous impact on the way people thought about current affairs as well as history. As Joshua Fogel and others have shown, when Chinese and Japanese historians met to discuss China's past, Marxism and Leninism often provided the common vocabulary.[56] Because this vocabulary was unambiguous regarding stages of historical development, scholars debated, for instance, the dates at which feudalism gave way to absolutism, and absolutism to capitalism, in a given society. In the famous controversy in Japan between those who interpreted the Meiji state as having been absolutist and those who argued that the Meiji Restoration had ushered in a period of bourgeois capitalism, the concepts and terms used by Japanese historians were those being employed by scholars elsewhere—another example of internationalization. Jawaharlal Nehru's autobiography, written in prison in 1934, similarly indicates that for him and for many others in India's nationalistic movement, not to mention communists, Marxism provided the ideological framework through which to understand what was happening to their society. The spread of Marxist historiography throughout the world provided terms and concepts that could be used by intellectuals, in a sense like Esperanto, to communicate with one another.[57]

Marxist terms and concepts were meant to challenge those of bourgeois historiography, but the two were not totally unrelated, at least not in the context of postwar internationalism. A good illustration of this is Stalin's little tract *Fundamentals of Leninism,* published in 1924. Although in this widely read booklet Stalin reiterated the Leninist thesis that "a handful of 'advanced countries'" was oppressing "the huge majority consisting of colonial and dependent countries," and that "true internationalism" had to be based on close relations among "the toiling masses" of all nations, he readily recognized that the conditions for such internationalism to emerge were becoming more favorable. This was because of the evolution of "a single chain called world economy" that linked national economies and possessions together. In such a situation, he observed, the masses could learn not only from "Russian revolutionary sweep" but also from "American efficiency"—the latter defined, in his words, as "that indomitable force which neither knows nor recognizes obstacles; which with its businesslike perseverance brushes aside all obstacles; which continues at a task once started until it is finished, even if it is a minor task; and without which serious constructive work is inconceivable."[58]

Such vocabulary could readily be understood by internationalists elsewhere—a fact that suggests the gap between liberal, bourgeois internationalism and radical, proletarian internationalism may not have been unbridgeable, for both looked to cross-national developments, particularly in the cultural realm, for clues to understanding the contemporary world. It is true that once the First Five-Year Plan was launched in the

Soviet Union, that country's espousal of internationalist perspectives weakened. But that did not prevent intellectuals
everywhere from continuing to view the Soviet Union as an
integral part, if not the center, of global dialogue. The signing,
by the Soviet Union as well as thirty-two other countries, of
the Pact of Paris in 1928, renouncing the use of force for the
solution of disputes, was symbolic of the coming together of
different strands of internationalism. Although a document
dealing more with legal, political internationalism than with
cultural internationalism, the Kellogg-Briand Pact should also
be put in the context of the energetic efforts by men and
women everywhere to construct a more interdependent
world, to open up people's minds so that they would understand one another a little better. Indeed, as Frank Ninkovich
has argued, to many supporters of the pact—in the United
States, women were particularly conspicuous among them—
the success of the treaty hinged on the operation of a world
public opinion. But world public opinion needed constant re-
inforcement and reeducation, and that was what the cultural
internationalists were trying to provide.[59]

Shortly after World War I, a Congressman from New York
remarked, "After preaching for thousands of years the father-
hood of God and the brotherhood of man, and then engaging
for five years in slaughter, it is but natural that we should be in
an abnormal state. While the killing of men's bodies has
stopped, the poisoning of minds has just begun."[60] An achievement such as the Kellogg-Briand Pact indicated, at least to the
internationalists of the 1920s, that men's minds were now a little less poisoned, a little more open to peaceful mutual interaction. Thanks to cultural internationalist movements and activities, many were willing to recognize that, in the words of

Manly O. Hudson, "all of the people of the world have been drawn into a single world community which bears little resemblance to the world of separate and self-contained states upon which the nineteenth century dawned."[61]

The history of the 1920s is often interpreted in terms of the rejection of internationalism and the resurgence of nationalism. In many areas of the world, it is true, forces that would develop into the excessive chauvinism of the subsequent decade were already evident in the first postwar decade. Moreover, countries in Europe, the Middle East, and Asia that were becoming sovereign entities consciously emphasized unique national traditions and cultures as part of their effort to develop a sense of nationhood. It is clear, nevertheless, that in the history of internationalism, the 1920s were memorable.

In *The History of Peace*, published in 1931, A.C.F. Beales gave detailed descriptions of various ideas of peace that had been developed since the eighteenth century and paid particular attention to the contributions made by the 1920s. He distinguished between "historical" and "philosophical" ideas of peace, the former being more grounded upon actual practices of diplomacy and the latter existing in the domain of ideals and visions. While Beales saw the chasm between the two as having remained as wide as ever, he might have been able, had he looked at the cultural internationalist movements, to see that the bridging of this gap was indeed what these movements were trying to accomplish. In this sense, H. G. Wells was more sensitive to contemporary trends when he noted, in 1930, that technological and economic developments were "forcing us towards the realisation of a single world community."[62]

Whether one followed Beales or Wells, or any number of

observers of the postwar scene, one might have concluded that movements for cosmopolitanism and cross-national communication were everywhere gaining momentum, and that there could be no turning around of this phenomenon, grounded as it was on modern innovations in communication, transportation, and information. Unfortunately, within but a short period of time, these innovations were to be put to use for brutal, diabolical ends in a changed world environment in which the gains of the 1920s would be all but nullified.

CHAPTER THREE

The Separation of Culture from Internationalism

The promising beginnings of cultural internationalism were dealt a crushing blow in the 1930s. The decade was characterized by forces that were the precise opposite of cultural internationalism: exclusionary nationalism, racism, aggression, and mass murder. Moreover, culture, instead of moderating national military power, was frequently combined with it, thereby losing its autonomy and its international character.

Nevertheless, the 1930s are worth studying in the history of modern internationalism—of all kinds—for a number of reasons. First, committed cultural internationalists never disappeared from the scene, and many of them continued their efforts against seemingly formidable obstacles. Second, these efforts were to have a major impact on internationalist activities once they were resumed after World War II. Third, despite the collapse of cultural and other types of internationalism in the 1930s, if anything cultural relations among nations came to be taken even more seriously by various governments than earlier. International cultural relations were actively promoted as much by totalitarian states as by the democracies. Indeed, this was the fundamental challenge faced by cultural internationalism. Cultural relations tended to be moored away from visions of an international community and anchored in formulations of national interest. In the process, the place of culture in international affairs underwent significant changes.

In some ways, cultural internationalism as a movement became even more active during the 1930s than in the 1920s. This may come as a surprise to those accustomed to viewing the 1930s as "nightmare years," to use William Shirer's graphic phrase.[1] How could the darkest decade in contemporary history—a decade that saw the Depression, the rise of totalitarianism, aggressive wars and atrocities, and countless instances of violence, sadism, and persecution—have seen anything but excessive nationalism, chauvinism, and racism? To introduce into the discussion of the 1930s, which began with Japan's defiance of the League of Nations and the failure of the major powers to coordinate their trade policies and ended with an alliance of European and Asian totalitarian states against the defenseless democracies, the theme of internationalism might appear like a futile and misguided exercise, if not a grave distortion of history.

It is because of the very resurgence of parochial forces in the 1930s—a fact of history beyond dispute—that one is struck by the efforts of internationalists to try, against all odds, to keep alive the flames of their hope. To be sure, internationalism in the age of economic nationalism and in an environment in which the League of Nations was fast losing its viability as an effective instrument for collective security, would not quite be the same thing as the internationalism of the 1920s. Moreover, as noted in the Introduction, the universalistic assumptions that had underlain internationalism after World War I came to be challenged by more self-conscious formulations of national cultures. Whereas in 1930 H. G. Wells could confidently assert that "the battle for the peace of the world is a battle for cosmopolitan ideas," during the 1930s fewer and fewer would be sanguine about such an assumption. For statesmen, publicists, intellectuals, and others struggling to preserve the peace, cosmopolitan ideals would appear unattainable, if not irrelevant. Nevertheless, amidst the turmoil caused by interstate rivalries and crises, Franklin D. Roosevelt could still declare that "civilization is not national—it is international."[2] So long as such an idea remained, the survival of cultural internationalism was a strong possibility.

Actually, the demise of internationalism was not a foreordained conclusion even in the 1930s, at least not until well into the decade. This was in part because the various internationalist projects and national organizations to promote them did not get started until the late 1920s, so that it was in the next decade that some of them achieved a measure of success. A good example was the International Institute for Intellectual Cooperation, established in Paris in 1926. It was primarily after 1930 that the institute emerged as a major center of cultural internationalism, thanks in no small measure to the leadership of a new director, Henri Bonnet. Prior to his appointment, there had been some criticism, especially abroad, of the ways in which institute affairs had been conducted. Because the French government had been the major donor of funds to the fledgling organization, there had been a tendency in France and elsewhere to view it as an instrument of French foreign policy. Bonnet, an educator and later France's ambassador to the United States, was determined to internationalize the activities of the institute and energetically promoted cross-national projects through national committees on intellectual cooperation in various countries. For instance, he was instrumental in starting a project for the translation of Spanish American literature into French and English, and in persuading some countries to establish collections of phonograph records ("gramophone record libraries") to bring together recordings of folk music and works by contemporary composers with a view to facilitating artistic exchanges.[3]

It is important to note that Bonnet's activities at the institute were carried on throughout the 1930s. It is true that in the new decade, in contrast to the preceding one, nationalism rather than internationalism once again became the predominant theme in the domestic and foreign affairs of most countries. Germany was but one extreme example of this shift. Before the coming to power of the Nazis in 1933, the Weimar Republic had been an ardent supporter of cultural internationalism (although, as Michael Burleigh and Wolfgang Wippermann have shown, even during the 1920s various organizations had existed to extol the virtues of patriotism, nationalism, and racism).[4] Weimar's cultivation, especially in the big cities, of cosmopolitanism had been remarkable. Expressed by innovative movements in music, art and architecture, the theater, and literature, its significance was not confined to one country. No less spectacular had been the willingness and efforts on the part of German academics, museum curators, artists, and others to join their counterparts elsewhere to promote cultural internationalism. Several of them had played key roles in the League of Nations Committee on Intellectual Cooperation, even before Germany was permitted to join the League in 1926.

All this changed virtually overnight once Adolf Hitler came to power. One after another, internationalist-oriented organizations in Germany were shut down, not least because Jews had been active in these organizations. The idea of one nation consisting of one race (*Volk*) was reiterated on every occasion; aliens (including Jews) were excluded from government, teaching, and other positions; internationalism came to be seen as the symbol of what had been wrong with Weimar culture; and young children were taught, as Hitler said, "nothing else but to think as Germans and to act as Germans."[5] It was not surprising that in December 1933 the Reich should have ordered the immediate cessation of all connections with the League's activities in intellectual cooperation, resulting in the resignation of leading German internationalists from the organizations in Geneva and Paris that were engaged in promoting cultural internationalism. Their departure was widely mourned, but there was little or nothing Germany's cultural internationalists could do in the changed atmosphere of the country. Many of them exiled themselves abroad, others cooperated with the Nazis with varying degrees of willingness, and a few spent the Nazi years in prison. (A notable example of the latter category was Carl von Ossietzky, a pacifist writer who was imprisoned in 1933 and was awarded a Nobel peace prize in 1935; the committee called him "a citizen of the world whose cause is freedom of thought, freedom of speech, and free competition in the realm of ideas." The Nazis forbade him to accept the award.) Some remained in Germany in the belief, as Wilhelm Furtwängler said in 1945, that their "remaining there is the best proof of the fact that there is still another Germany."[6] Schools, universities, and even families continued to host foreign students. Individuals risked their lives to promote internationalism through their private initiatives. We will never know the exact number of these latter, and the survival of some form of cultural internationalism in Germany in the 1930s awaits monographic treatment.

It is clear, in any event, that Nazi Germany rejected the internationalist tendencies of the 1920s. Political, literary, and artistic themes again stressed state, nation, war, and self-sacrifice for the good of the community. In war, wrote the novelist Edgar Maass, "a man sacrifices himself for another. . . . The millions who died in war have fulfilled once again a great and eternal law."[7] This was in sharp contrast to earlier writings that had stressed the meaninglessness of fighting against other human beings and connected the individual to the whole of humanity without the intermediation of the national community. Now the nation returned to the fore—a community in which past, present, and future were intimately linked. Thus Joachim von der Boltz characterized war as a trial; justice and strength, generated by war, would cleanse the old and restore faith in youth. Young men steeled by war would "run over peace" like a storm in spring and brush away all deceit and false, hollow values.[8] Ernest Röhm, commander of the Storm Troopers (S.A.) until he was assassinated at Hitler's instigation in 1934, wrote, "War awakens and strengthens the best forces of the nation. . . . For the soldier, war is the foundation of youth, hope, and fulfillment."[9] There was little room in such expressions for an interdependent, cooperative world community. Rather, international affairs were once again seen as an arena for conflict, not necessarily in the traditional geopolitical formulations (although these were never absent from German foreign policy), but in terms of the clash of races and cultures, categories that were considered to be immutable.

That was one of the most serious challenges to internationalism in the interwar years. If races and cultures were immutable, what point was there in trying to bring them together to promote mutual communication? What point in aspiring to transform ideas and ways of life so as to enlarge the spheres in which peoples and nations could cooperate? From the perspective of the German ideologues and their counterparts elsewhere in the 1930s, such attempts were not only doomed to failure but also pernicious, standing in the way of "eternal necessities."

The assault on cultural internationalism was not confined to Nazi Germany, nor was it a product of racism alone. The Soviet Union, which might have been expected to oppose itself to the cultural and racial nationalism of Germany, was similarly turning against internationalism, indicating that the resurgence of nationalistic mentalities and the stifling of internationalist forces was a widespread phenomenon in the 1930s. The vibrant and innovative cultural movements that had been evident in post-Revolutionary Russia gave way, during the era of Stalinist dictatorship, to xenophobia and geopolitics. To be sure, Moscow's call for a worldwide anti-fascist front, enunciated at the 1935 Comintern congress, had cultural implications, to bring cultural and intellectual leaders of various countries together against the barbarism of Nazi policies. The "international writers' congress for the defense of culture," held in Paris in the same year, was a good example. André Gide, Aldous Huxley, Ilya Ehrenberg, and many other intellectuals attended and proclaimed their "defense of culture" against the Nazi assault on the cultural heritage. Although different from League-initiated cultural initiatives, Comintern-sponsored efforts, like those of the League, indicated the willingness on the part of artists and intellectuals to maintain contact and promote the cause of internationalism. (It is worth noting that one of the Comintern's major publications, *World Culture*, a monthly journal, was translated into many languages and kept

alive the vision of an international cultural movement.) Unfortunately, this phase of Comintern internationalism did not
last. As Robert Tucker has shown, it was superseded by a cultural nationalism that became incorporated into a geopolitically oriented Stalinist policy, eventuating in the Nazi-Soviet
nonaggression pact of 1939. Intellectual and cultural figures
with ties to foreign lands became suspect, and many of them
were persecuted simply because they knew too much about the
world.[10]

Contemporary observers used words like cultural decom-
position (Leon Trotsky) and disintegration (Reinhold Niebuhr) to describe these phenomena. As Niebuhr noted in an
aptly titled book, *Reflections on the End of an Era* (1934), one
era, characterized by liberalism and peace, had ended, to be replaced by a long period in which "the anarchic, the demonic
and the primeval in man's collective behavior" were likely to
be the dominant themes. Referring to the deepening economic
crisis and the rise of totalitarianism in Europe, the American
theologian gloomily noted that the West "lives under the peril
of a new war which it seems powerless to avert and it suffers
from serious dislocations in its economic processes which it
cannot overcome. Though it is generally known that another
war will prove suicidal to the whole of western culture, it is no
longer certain that fear of the possibility of such a suicide will
avert the war."[11] There was evidently a "spiritual crisis" in Europe, as Janet Flanner noted in her *New Yorker* columns, and
the sense of global interdependence was one of the first casu-
alties of this crisis. (The "days of civilized, uncensored plea-
sures" of the 1920s, Flanner wrote in 1939, were now remem-
bered in sorrow. The cultural abyss of the 1930s "was enough
to make the angels weep.")[12]

Even the nontotalitarian states were abandoning their pro-
fessed ideals of internationalism for the pragmatic needs of
national interest. Their economic policies, ranging from protec-
tionism to preferential trade agreements, from barter arrangements to currency devaluation, were adopted without regard
to the stability of international commercial and financial affairs, and certainly with little regard for the implications of
such nationalistic policies for international cultural endeavors.
The result was a crisis of "capitalist internationalism," as
William Y. Elliott noted as early as 1932.[13] National salvation,
not international cooperation, was the theme stressed in the
democracies as well as in antidemocratic states. In an extremely penetrating observation of the U.S. scene in the early
1930s, *America in Search of Culture* (1933), William A. Orton
noted that amid the pervasive sense of disillusion and doubt,
Americans might yet find out that "there is a very deep connection between one's nation and one's inner life."[14] The rediscovery of nationalism as the key to coping with the economic, political, and spiritual crises of the day had obvious
implications for the future of internationalism. In the United
States, this trend has been carefully documented by Warren
Susman, Richard Pells, and others. They have noted, for instance, that American intellectuals, struggling with the problem of regaining spiritual strength after the seeming collapse
of familiar ideas and assumptions, came to stress "the American way of life," the American tradition, and American civilization as one possible realm of certainty and continuity.[15]
Together with other contemporary movements like neutral-
ism, pacifism, and noninterventionism, such a phenomenon indicated that in one respect the resurgence of nationalism was a
widespread phenomenon, not just a malaise of totalitarian states.

It is all the more remarkable, therefore, that in a global environment where nationalistic trends were threatening to undermine, even obliterate, ideals of international cooperation and cross-national communication, efforts should have continued to be made by dedicated internationalists to continue their activities, particularly in the cultural sphere. Rather than giving up, the League's Intellectual Cooperation Committee, for instance, intensified its efforts, even when the League itself was proving ineffectual in the political arena. Intellectual leaders and cultural-exchange personnel from many countries worked assiduously, as if to remind the world that there still was room for an international agency even at a time when militant nationalism appeared to be returning with a vengeance, and that, if the agency could do little to prevent the horrors of war and aggression, it could at least preserve itself as a witness to the nobler instincts of humanity.

In the fall of 1931, as Japanese forces began the conquest of Manchuria, Intellectual Cooperation representatives from Poland, Britain, and Germany proposed the convening of a "world conference on training in world citizenship." In order to develop "the spirit of international cooperation," the proposers said, it was imperative to improve the teaching of history, geography, and related subjects.[16] The proposal was duly forwarded to various countries' committees on intellectual cooperation. In the meantime, the League held a conference "for the protection and preservation of artistic and historical monuments." Somewhat in the spirit of the International Flag movement (noted in chapter 2), the conferees laid down the principle that "in this matter, as in others, the peoples are interdependent . . . and that this interdependence must give rise to a new form of international cooperation." Although the conference stopped short of actually making up a list of artistic objects to be protected in wartime, the fact that such a meeting took place in the middle of the Depression deserves notice. In 1934, to cite another example of a theme continuing on from the 1920s, an international conference on the teaching of history was held in Basel to discuss "ways in which history teaching can promote international understanding." An official of the Institute for Intellectual Cooperation participating in the gathering endorsed the idea that "textbook authors should deal, in addition to national histories, with . . . the joint work of civilisation and the growing interdependence of nations."[17] As late as 1935, French and German teachers were meeting to continue their discussion of textbook revision as a joint enterprise.[18]

It may be that student and scholarly exchanges across nations became even more widespread in the 1930s than in the preceding decade. In 1934, "the committee of representatives of students' international organizations" met in Paris and reaffirmed the need for strengthening bonds among students of all countries.[19] The League of Nations was particularly interested in promoting exchanges between Europeans and Chinese, sending more than forty technical, educational, and cultural relations specialists to various parts of China. Those going included Henri Bonnet, R. H. Tawney, and Ludwik Rajchman. China, in turn, sent about eighty individuals to study public health, hydraulic engineering, and other subjects at European universities and research centers. In late 1932 and early 1933, six Chinese educators visited Poland, Germany, France, Britain, Italy, Austria, and the Soviet Union under League auspices to initiate educational exchanges with these countries. These activities—undertaken, it should be noted, in the midst of an armed conflict with Japan in the Northeast—resulted in 1933 in the establishment of a Chinese committee on intellectual cooperation in Shanghai. The organization kept in close touch with more than five hundred educational and scholarly institutions in China, as well as with their counterparts abroad.[20]

Meantime, also in 1933, the French government launched a program for hosting Japanese university graduates for graduate study. A number of *boursiers* were sent to Paris after a rigorous competition, some of whom were to stay in the host country till the end of World War II. American and Japanese students, on their part, started holding annual conferences for the exchange of information and opinion. Established in 1934, these conferences continued to be held right up to the eve of the war.[21] Throughout the 1930s, the Edgar A. Bancroft Foundation, created to honor the memory of a former U.S. ambassador to Japan, sent one Japanese student each year to a U.S. college. An American educator, Donald Watt, initiated a program in 1932 for sending teenagers to Europe to experience "international living." The Experiment in International Living, although started in the middle of the Depression, thrived, with American boys and girls living with host families in Britain, France, Germany, Austria, Norway, Sweden, and Italy. American families, in turn, hosted "Experimenters" from these countries.[22]

The International Bureau of Education, established in Geneva in 1929 to "act as an information centre for all matters relating to Education," continued to grow in the 1930s and by 1938 totaled forty-three members, including Germany, Italy, France, Spain, Switzerland, Poland, Czechoslovakia, Japan, Egypt, Argentina, and Ecuador. The bureau's permanent exhibition, at Geneva, contained textbooks and statistics on education as well as "syllabuses and timetables of the subjects taught." (It is noteworthy that, on the eve of the war, Germany was represented on the bureau, through the Central Institute for Education and Lessons; whereas Britain refused to join on the grounds that British participation would not "have any very great propaganda value," as an August 1938 Foreign Office memorandum put it.)[23] As late as 1934, the International All Peoples Association, chaired by Sir Evelyn Wrench—"a society of men and women, belonging to all nations, which seeks to remove prejudice and misunderstanding between the peoples of the world"—maintained libraries of British books in five German cities as well as in Rome, Paris, Brussels, the Hague, Vienna, Budapest, Stockholm, and Riga.[24] In 1938, according to a report by the International Institute for Intellectual Cooperation, more translations from foreign-language books were published in Germany (782) than in the United States (317) or the United Kingdom (317).[25]

Such scattered examples, of course, do not amount to sustained efforts at cultural internationalism, and it would be easy to dismiss them as expressions of dilettantism or at best naive idealism that made little or no impact on the "realities" of international affairs. But, whatever their cumulative impact, they are as much part of the historical record as the Japanese aggression in China, the German decision to rearm, and other events that were steadily undermining the structure of the world community. In a recent book on France during the 1930s, Eugen Weber notes that a "book about the thirties must be, directly or indirectly, about the wounds and mind-set of a host of survivors—veterans, widows, orphans, parents—grieving for the slaughtered and determined to avoid a repeat performance of the disaster."[26] Precisely because these men and women were the central figures in the history of the 1930s, and because their prayers were to be unheeded, it is important to pay close attention to the countless valiant attempts, of which international cultural activities formed an essential part, throughout the decade that sought to find an alternative to another disastrous war. These efforts provided a link between the world of the 1920s and the world that came after World War II.

Cultural internationalist activities in the 1930s were not confined to art preservation, textbook revision, and student and scholarly exchanges. In the early part of the decade, the concept of "outlawry of war" that had been translated into the 1928 Kellogg-Briand Pact was provided with cultural underpinnings when it was redefined as "moral disarmament." Despite the fact that Japan had violated the pact by its aggression in Manchuria and that the world disarmament conference, convened in Geneva in 1932, was getting nowhere, civilian and intellectual leaders in many countries—including those from Japan and Germany—pushed for the idea that "the success of military disarmament . . . calls for moral disarmament." Indeed, the Geneva disarmament conference included an agenda on moral disarmament, the assumption being that no technical limitation on the sizes of armed forces would ensure peace unless it were backed up by a habit of mind that was less chauvinistic and more cosmopolitan. The committee of scientific advisors attached to the League noted that a successful world disarmament program depended on the efforts of civilian officials and military officers everywhere—people who had spent their years of training abroad and so become "soldiers of peace and friends of intellectual cooperation." The committee on moral disarmament, an official part of the Geneva conference, insisted that military disarmament must be coupled with the rewriting of school textbooks in many countries that seemed to exhibit a spirit of animosity toward one another.[27]

Of course, neither military nor moral disarmament was achieved in 1932, but the internationalists did not give up. It is a striking feature of cultural internationalism in the 1930s (or what was left of it) that it came to be vigorously pushed by representatives of such countries as Poland, Egypt, China, and Brazil, as if to make up for the departure of Germans from the scene and the expected defection (though it did not materialize right away) of Japanese, Italians, and others from international cultural activities. Precisely because so many parts of the world were coming under the control of dictatorships and aggressive regimes that stifled open cultural expression and communication, the significance of cultural internationalism seemed to increase: it became a keeper of the vision of freedom that might some day return to those lands. A 1934 League of Nations report on intellectual cooperation noted, "The more the nations of the world are forced to retire into themselves, the more strongly the divisions between the peoples will be felt and the greater the need for intellectual union and collaboration." A report by the Paris Institute insisted that "at a time when, in the political sphere, spiritual life is menaced by the instability of international relations, by the consequent hesitation and anxieties and by the hazards of production and the crises through which the economic system is passing, [there is] a keener realization of the need of the peoples of the world to know and understand one another." Efforts at intellectual cooperation were more than ever necessary to ensure "the recognition of a universal moral doctrine [and] the prevention of the dangerous excesses and warped mentality that are born of hatred."[28]

Dangerous excesses and warped mentalities were, unfortunately, to be the rule in most parts of the world throughout the rest of the decade. But that did not prevent the vision from being preserved in many lands and being constantly reiterated through the League and other agencies. In a remarkable coincidence, on July 7, 1937, the day when fighting broke out between Chinese and Japanese forces at Marco Polo bridge near Peking—a clash that was to develop into a full-scale war on the Asian continent lasting more than eight years—a small group of Chinese and Japanese educators were meeting in Geneva with their colleagues from thirty-seven other countries to discuss the current status of and future possibilities for intellectual cooperation. While their armies clashed, intellectual leaders from the two countries—prominent scholars like Li Yu-ying from China and Anesaki Masaharu from Japan—continued to engage in a discussion that concerned the whole world, "The Immediate Future of Letters." They joined other eminent intellectuals—among them Paul Valéry, Gilbert Murray, Thornton Wilder, Jacob Huizinga, Georges Duhamel, and Paul Hazard—and their participation on this occasion struck one observer as evidence that "striving after universality . . . is one of the essential features of intellectual cooperation," which in turn was a necessary condition of internationalism.[29]

Such conversations did nothing to stop the war in China; moreover, not all educators and intellectuals in China and Japan were committed internationalists like Li and Anesaki, any more than were their counterparts elsewhere. It is all the more remarkable, then, that some, at least, did not give up their devotion to cultural internationalism. In an impressive reaffirmation of this movement, representatives at the "Future of Letters" conference in Geneva that summer of 1937 adopted a "draft act on intellectual cooperation." The signatories, from thirty-nine countries, were conscious of their "common interest in preserving mankind's heritage of culture and in promoting the further development of the sciences, arts and letters." They believed that "the cause of peace would be served by the promotion of cultural relations between peoples through an intellectual body having a threefold character of universality, permanence and independence."[30] This last point reflected the sense shared by the participants that an international body even more strongly committed to these principles than the League's Committee on Intellectual Cooperation or its Paris counterpart would be needed to cope with the crisis of the 1930s and that such an organization required much more substantial funding than the existing agencies. An extremely idealistic proposal in an age when "realism," cynicism, and geopolitics were again holding sway, it nevertheless drew the support of some governments—France, Poland, Czechoslovakia, and a number of Latin American countries. Unfortunately, soon some of these countries would be occupied by German forces and the rest enveloped in another world war. But the very existence of such a movement was laying the groundwork for what would reappear after the war in the form of the United Nations Educational, Scientific, and Cultural Organization (UNESCO).

The next full meeting of the International Committee on Intellectual Cooperation was held in Geneva in July 1939. As the delegates sensed that another war was coming in Europe, Gilbert Murray declared that "if the worse came to the worst—if the material structure of civilisation were destroyed by war—intellectual values would still not perish . . . the Committee would have saved something in the sphere of arts and letters, something in the field of mathematics and pure science, something, too, in the realm of charity and goodwill towards mankind."[31] Perhaps the best expression of the cultural internationalist faith when such faith appeared about to be drowned in yet another burst of nationalistic emotions, these words were echoed a few weeks later, as war came. On September 4, the day after war was declared by Britain and France against Germany in retaliation against the latter's invasion of Poland, Henri Bonnet, head of the Paris Institute for Intellectual Cooperation, sent out a circular to more than a thousand organizations and individuals who had worked with him on behalf of cultural internationalism. He told them that he and his colleagues in France were determined to continue their efforts. He was even then making preparations for another gathering of representatives of the various national committees on intellectual cooperation, to take place in Paris in 1940.[32]

Of course, no such meeting was to be held, and Bonnet soon had to flee Paris for Bordeaux and then for London. He wound up in the United States in 1941, where he energetically carried on his mission, giving lectures on cultural exchange and establishing personal contact with Americans who shared his vision. It was not surprising, given his visibility and obvious commitment to internationalism, that in 1944 he should be chosen by Charles de Gaulle to represent liberated France as its ambassador in the United States.

By the time Bonnet arrived in the United States, the latter had become perhaps the nation most actively promoting cultural internationalism. The revival of internationalism in the United States in the 1930s is an interesting phenomenon that has not received the attention it deserves. As noted earlier, the intellectual climate during the early years of the Depression was not conducive to internationalism. Apart from the individuals and organizations, such as those mentioned above, that continued their heroic efforts on behalf of student exchange and related programs, it may well be that for many Americans still interested in working for internationalist causes, the Soviet Union appeared to provide the best solution. Thousands from the United States went there to help with the First Five-Year Plan (1928–32) and its sequel. A large number of prominent American intellectuals considered the world's future lay in noncapitalist alternatives exemplified by the Soviet model, and many joined the Moscow-inspired international movement to fight for the Spanish republic against the fascist insurgents. It is true that these activities were more in the political than in the cultural realm, and the Soviet-led internationalism in the 1930s was clearly intended for checking the growth of Nazi Germany's and militarist Japan's aggressive power.

Even so, Americans (as well as others) who supported the Comintern's anti-fascist "popular front" strategy were keenly aware of the intellectual and ideological dimension of the movement. As Malcolm Cowley, one of the American supporters of the popular front, has written in his reminiscences of the 1930s, "Like the Russians . . . and like many American intellectuals at the time, I insisted on thinking in terms of either-or: either peace in the world that was ruled by workers or war between rival imperialisms."[33] In other words, either nationalistic rivalries would prevail, or else a new internationalism would have to emerge on the basis of worker solidarity under the leadership of the Comintern. Few went that far, and even Cowley and like-minded intellectuals in time came to reject that solution; nevertheless, it is important to note that to many in the United States and elsewhere the Comintern-inspired internationalism offered not just a political strategy to resist fascist aggression but also a way of thought, an internationalist vocabulary, at a time when few alternatives to nationalism appeared to be available. The Soviet Union, rather than the League of Nations or any other entity, appeared to hold out the best hope for internationalism.

The influence of the Soviet Union in promoting internationalism, cultural and otherwise, steadily waned, however, as in the late 1930s the Stalinist regime reverted to geopolitical nationalism. Even the Comintern's erstwhile supporters such as Cowley and, to cite perhaps the most famous example, George Orwell, whose *Homage to Catalonia* (1937) was a record of his disillusionment, lost their enthusiasm. Apart from a few who continued to believe in, and work for, the Comintern, in effect becoming intelligence agents on behalf of the Soviet Union, most began to look elsewhere. It was then that the United States, moving in the opposite direction, began to shed its nationalistic outlook and champion the cause of internationalism—political, economic, and cultural.

Although the U.S. rediscovery and reaffirmation of internationalism coincided with a shift, however slow at first, in official policy, away from the unilateral pursuit of national interests to the forging of international cooperation, we should not forget that the reemergence of cultural internationalism in the United States was facilitated by the patient and persevering efforts of U.S. internationalists who, like their European counterparts, had tried to keep alive the vision and the dream. They—individuals like James Shotwell, who continued to operate the national committee on intellectual cooperation from an office in the Columbia University Faculty Club—were there when the need arose to provide ideas and staff support for the government's internationalist projects. Studies of non-Western cultures continued to be promoted in U.S. universities in the belief, as a 1935 report for the Rockefeller Foundation put it, that "the counteragent to . . . artificial patriotic sensitization is familiarity with many cultures." Echoing the sentiments prevalent during the 1920s, the report asserted, "Nationalism cannot resist the force of powerful intellectual curiosities that carry individuals beyond all borders to common sources of knowledge."[34] Some, at least, Roman Catholic leaders in the United States reacted against the nationalistic tendencies of the time by reaffirming the bonds existing among all members of the church. As Fulton Sheen wrote in 1935, "the Eucharist dissolves all boundaries, nationalities and races into a supernatural fellowship where all men are brothers of the Divine Son and adopted sons of the Heavenly Father."[35] Clearly, such ideas kept alive visions of universalism and prepared the ground for the U.S. government's active pursuit of internationalist agendas.

A very good example, and one of the earliest instances, of official U.S. internationalism was the Buenos Aires conference of American states, held at the end of 1936. The conferees set up a system of government-sponsored student exchange programs.[36] The agreement resulted in the coming to U.S. colleges and universities of nearly one thousand students from Central and South America, and, in turn, the sending of about a hundred U.S. students to those regions. This was the first officially sponsored student exchange program between American states, and it indicated that, in the United States, no longer only private individuals and organizations but officials had become interested in the idea of cultural exchange. At the

Buenos Aires conference, five out of eleven conventions and treaties signed dealt with cultural matters. But such agreements would have remained on paper if there had not been a network of internationalist individuals and organizations ready to step in and implement these programs. As seen in chapter 2, some of the Latin American countries had been avid promoters of cultural internationalism, and they were now eager to join the United States in expanding projects for cultural exchange. At the next gathering of American states, held in Lima in 1938, one-third of the resolutions introduced dealt with inter-American intellectual cooperation. And in the following year, representatives from the intellectual cooperation committees of the United States, Argentina, Bolivia, Brazil, Chile, Cuba, the Dominican Republic, Ecuador, Haiti, Mexico, Peru, El Salvador, and Uruguay came together to discuss ways to further the cause in a world seemingly turning more and more against cooperative effort.[37]

The establishment, in 1938, of the division of cultural relations within the State Department suggested that for virtually the first time (if one excepted the Boxer indemnity program for bringing Chinese students to U.S. colleges), cultural internationalist activities were becoming an arena for close cooperation between the U.S. government and the public. Ben M. Cherrington, the first director of the new office, had been active in YMCA work: instrumental in organizing seminars in Europe after the war, he had also promoted adult education programs in international affairs in Denver. After serving in the new State Department post for two years, he left Washington to return to the University of Denver, where he designed a course on "the function of cultural interchange in international relations."[38] This may well have been one of the first such courses anywhere in the United States. (In 1941, Cherrington admitted that it was very difficult to find sufficient reading material for the course.) He was followed at the State Department by Charles Thomson, another ardent advocate of inter-American cultural exchange, and the two kept up a correspondence. Through them and other like-minded individuals, as Robert David Johnson has shown, cultural internationalism in the United States steadily gained momentum.[39]

To cite an example from the activities of Cherrington, Thomson, and other cultural internationalists, in 1940 Cherrington proposed to the State Department that a systematic program for an exchange of visitors between the United States and Latin American countries be initiated. Such visits, be-lieved, "would diffuse a type of mutual understanding and appreciation which cannot be gained through the usual avenue of communication and public information." Rather than leaving such an important project to normal tourism, Cherrington believed that professional and service organizations in the United States should be asked to select and send citizens to other American republics and, on their part, receive visitors from these countries. The U.S. government would sponsor such a program to the extent of providing transportation and defraying the administrative expenses of an agency to be set up for carrying out the project. In the meantime, Cherrington considered it important to expand cultural exchange programs to other parts of the world. In April 1941, for instance, he wrote to Thomson suggesting the desirability of launching cultural relations projects with Canada and with China.[40] These proposals met with the warm endorsement of the State Department. The war in Europe and the approaching conflict in Asia made the implementation of such projects in the immediate future problematical, but it is important to note that there was active interchange between private agencies and the government in developing agendas for cultural international-ism. What may be termed the "cultural-exchange commu-nity" was fast taking shape.

Of course, governmental support for, and sponsorship of, cultural internationalism would inevitably affect the nature of the movement. Officially sanctioned and promoted, cultural internationalism would become an aspect, an agent, of foreign policy. Cultural diplomacy, rather than cultural international-ism, might be the correct term to use for such activity. As Frank Ninkovich has argued, in the United States the official endorsement of international cultural activities created a ten-sion in a society that had traditionally considered cultural pur-suits to be strictly private affairs in which the state would not, and should not, intervene.[41] Once culture came to be seen as a concern of the state, it could lose its autonomy. Governmen-tally sponsored cultural projects might not necessarily be those that private individuals and foundations considered impor-tant; conversely, private initiatives might not fit into official cultural agendas and might even be viewed as subversive of foreign policy.

These are questions in which cultural historians have shown increasing interest. They have argued, in effect, that at any given moment in a nation's history a certain cultural defini-tion and identity are imposed on the society by those who hold power in such matters, thus "centering" cultural activi-ties in an officially sanctioned manner. In a society as hetero-geneous as the United States, it would be difficult to apply such a formula simplistically, but cultural historians have as-serted that it is possible to identify certain hegemonic constructions of culture, whether they are produced by the state, by the elites, or by both (in a "corporatist" arrangement of state-elite cooperation). Whatever the merits of such an argument, it would be of crucial importance to recognize changes over time: that the way in which culture becomes "centered" varies from period to period. In our context, it is pertinent to ask not just how hegemonic cultures were defined but why the government felt the need to step into the picture. Why did official Washington, whose foreign policy had been by and large minimalist during the 1930s, now decide to reformulate it so as to include the cultural dimension?

Clearly, officials were broadening the scope of foreign policy. Hitherto predominantly defined by economic issues, U.S. foreign relations were having to cope with the mounting tensions in Europe and Asia created by the aggressive behavior of the totalitarian states. The most obvious response to this crisis, to be sure, was geopolitical, involving economic mobilization and military preparedness. This had little to do with cultural internationalism as such; if anything, the resurgence of geopolitical realism in the late 1930s could have resulted in the stifling of the efforts in the cultural arena. (To complicate the picture further, the increasing vogue for geopolitics in U.S. thought was itself a product of "the intellectual migration"— the coming of European scholars, literary figures, journalists, and others to the United States to escape European totalitarianism.[42] A number of these Europeans found refuge in influential academic settings—Yale, Princeton, Chicago, to cite prominent examples—and began holding seminars and writing books on statecraft, strategy, alliance diplomacy, and the like in a "realist" vein, to counter what they considered the still prevailing "idealism" of Americans when viewing international affairs.) In any event, the primacy of security and military considerations in United States strategy at the end of the decade could have overwhelmed the cultural dimension of foreign policy, but for the fact that both officials and opinion leaders believed the threat posed to world peace and national interests was not just military and economic, but was also cultural and ideological.

To respond to that challenge, it was considered extremely important to reaffirm a faith in democracy and liberalism in the United States, following their having been discredited and undermined during the first years of the Depression. But more would be needed: the United States would have to influence world opinion away from totalitarianism toward a more open, humane perspective on life. This was essentially a traditional American perspective, one that had been reinforced by Wilsonianism. But the legacy of postwar internationalism provided a ready vehicle for implementing such an ideological counteroffensive. International relations after 1919 had developed theories and practices of cultural internationalism that, while eclipsed during the Depression decade, could be resurrected and put at the service of official foreign policy. One sees here an unmistakable impact of the 1920s on the 1930s; postwar international relations had been so strongly affected by the cultural dimension that, when international tensions arose in the 1930s, various governments, instead of merely reverting to power politics, sought to appropriate this aspect of foreign relations, to make use of it as a means for promoting their strategies.

There is little doubt that in thus becoming an object of foreign policy more explicitly than in the 1920s, cultural internationalism inevitably changed its character. To be sure, the earlier ideal of promoting cross-national communication as a

means for establishing a more peaceful world order continued
to be carried on, though by a dwindling number of die-hard
internationalists, such as Bonnet, but cultural diplomacy, officially sanctioned and implemented, was now the norm. But,
whatever form it took, culture remained very much at the core
of international affairs, even as nations braced themselves in
anticipation of war. In much the same way that the definition
of peace had been broadened in the 1920s through cultural internationalist activities, the foreign policies of the powers as
they prepared for war in the 1930s revealed an awareness of the
role of cultural communication and influence across national
boundaries. Cultural "borderlands" did not shrink or close in
that sense. It may even be said that in the 1930s, usually characterized as a decade of nationalistic excesses and geopolitical
realism, culture came to count far more than ever before as a
factor in international relations.

Examples from two other countries will further shed light
on this phenomenon. In an interesting coincidence, in 1934
both Britain and Japan established semiofficial institutions
whose mandate was to provide cultural underpinnings for
their respective foreign policies. The Foreign Office in London initiated the founding of the British Council for Relations
with Other Countries, an organization whose mission was
viewed by government officials as more unambiguously "cultural propaganda" than the national committee on intellectual
cooperation. Alarmed at the rising popularity of Nazism and
fascism in Europe, the government in London was eager from
earlier on to engage in a cultural diplomacy through the dissemination of British books, ideas, and even the arts. At one
point, the Foreign Office toyed with the idea of making use of
the All Peoples Association's foreign libraries for this end, but

decided to establish a new organization specifically designed for cultural propaganda purposes.

The seriousness with which the government took the project may be seen in the fact that, whereas the Foreign Office's annual subsidy to the national committee on intellectual cooperation had diminished to a mere £150 after 1933, on the grounds that the national economic crisis made such a cut necessary, it gave the British Council an initial grant of £5,000. Clearly, London's intention was to promote other countries' understanding of British culture and society; as seen, for instance, in an ambitious project to send British musicians to Eastern Europe (they were touring Czechoslovakia on the eve of the Munich conference) and to hold an international congress of musicians in England.[43] The idea was to make use of such cultural exchange programs as an important part of foreign policy. These programs, it was believed, were now becoming more than ever pertinent in view of the social and cultural transformations abroad. At a time when extremist influences appeared to be spreading all over the world, it was considered imperative to counter the trend through Britain's own cultural undertakings.

For a Foreign Office that had traditionally shown little interest in cultural affairs to engage in such activities was an excellent indication of the changed nature of international affairs in the 1930s. As in the United States, in Britain, too, the government began to consider cultural pursuits too important to be left entirely in private hands. (It is interesting to note that, when the thirtieth Esperanto congress was convened in London in the summer of 1938, the British government took the view that "it is undesirable to support organisations which have as their object the encouragement of artificial languages, when we are seeking to secure the adoption of English as the second language in all foreign countries."[44] Such a frank admission confirmed both official involvement in cultural affairs and the importance of culture in foreign policy, two key themes of international relations in the 1930s.)

Japan's counterpart to the British Council, Kokusai Bunka Shinkōkai (KBS—or the Society for International Cultural Relations), was also a product of initiatives by a foreign ministry. By then, Japan's military conquest of Manchuria was complete, and there had been incursions into north China. These aggressions were denounced by Chinese intellectuals as a cultural assault on their nation. In 1932, for instance, Ts'ai Yüan-p'ei, president of Academia Sinica, complained to the League of Nations that Japanese warplanes had aimed their bombs at Chinese museums, libraries, publishing houses, and schools, as if to seek to obliterate cultural and educational activities in China. Ts'ai called on "the intellectual leaders of the world" to condemn "such barbarity of the Japanese military in destroying China's educational and cultural organs." What was barbarity in Chinese eyes was defended as "an unparalleled act of cultural preservation" by Japan, whose army removed some eight hundred thousand books from libraries in Shanghai and Nanking in 1937: an official spokesman stated that these books ultimately would be returned to China "in order to contribute to the advancement of East Asian culture."[45]

This was one of the more grotesque examples of the cultural aspect of the Asian war, and it may well be wondered if such activities did not make the concept of culture overly malleable, if not meaningless. At one level this was certainly the case. "Cultural operations," as the Japanese termed their action in Manchuria and the rest of China, had nothing to do with cultural internationalism but were part and parcel of the war of conquest. At another level, however, it is pertinent to ask why the Japanese bothered to talk of culture and cultural relations at all when they were engaged in acts of aggression. The military conquest of Manchuria was accompanied, from the outset, by an ambitious occupation policy that sought to influence, if not totally control, the educational, intellectual, and cultural life of the people—the so-called five races: Chinese, Manchurians, Mongolians, Koreans, and Japanese—in the vast expanse of northeast China. The Japanese occupiers talked of establishing a "paradise" in Manchuria—a self-serving notion designed to distinguish Japanese from other powers' imperialism. But the very rhetoric revealed a determination to reshape the region's society and culture, and efforts were made to open many primary schools and adult education classes, as well as a central university for the education of residents. According to a propaganda leaflet, the university, Shinkyō Daigaku (Hsinching University), aimed at producing "pioneering leaders in the establishment of a moral world." The Japanese in Manchuria stressed that they were developing a new culture, different from Western civilization and designed for "the awakening of Asia."[46] To this end, not only schools but facilities for popular culture, such as movie studios and printing presses, were created. Architectural monuments were built to illustrate the new culture.

Likewise, when Japanese forces began invading north China, one of the first acts was the establishment of Hsinmin Hui, or "new people's associations," joint Chinese-Japanese cultural organizations for the promotion of Asian culture. At Hsinmin schools, students and adults were taught to awaken themselves to their Asian identity and shed the influence of the allegedly bankrupt Western civilization.[47] The number of Chinese who cooperated in the undertaking was very small, perhaps less than one percent of the population of the occupied areas, but Japanese intellectuals and officials took the task with utmost seriousness. As was observed by Fujisawa Chikao, an erstwhile official of the League of Nations who in the 1930s became a leading apologist for Japanese imperialism on the continent, nations were groping for new cultural principles, and it was Japan's mission to provide an answer. According to Fujisawa, the internationalism he had witnessed through League activities had been derived from Western liberalism, which then was imposed on the rest of the world. Now, he argued, Japan must establish the basis for a more just pattern of international relations built on the principles of harmony and trust.[48]

As such statements revealed, the Japanese were anxious to couch their foreign policy, including their aggressive wars on the continent, on a cultural foundation. Prime Minister Konoe Fumimaro's declaration on November 3, 1938, for the establishment of a new order in East Asia stated that Japan, Manchukuo (the occupied northeast), and China were to "create a new culture and realize close economic cohesion throughout East Asia." Culture here was clearly a parochial notion, not a concept that suggested the sharing of common values and aspirations throughout the world. Rather, it pitted Japanese, and Asian, ways of life and thought against those of the West. Culture was an instrument of imperialism, not of internationalism. (Imperialism and internationalism may have overlapped at the beginning of the century, as suggested earlier, but no longer.)

The fact remains that the Japanese were eager to see cultural implications in what they were doing and to promote the cultural aspect of their foreign affairs throughout the 1930s. Although the bulk of cultural relations activities were carried out in China, they were by no means confined to the Asian continent.

From the beginning, KBS was interested in promoting exchanges with other countries. It took over many of the functions of Japan's national committee for intellectual cooperation and engaged in such activities as the exchange of visitors with foreign countries and the establishment of Japanese libraries abroad—projects very similar to those being undertaken by the British Council. Cultural exchange agreements were signed with Germany, in 1938, and Italy, in 1939. The German-Japanese agreement on cultural cooperation stated that the two nations recognized the importance of strengthening their close ties through cultural relations. Japanese culture, the document said, was based on the nation's "unique spirit," and German culture was a product of "the racial and national life of Germany."[49] How such essentialist formulations of their respective cultures could promote mutual understanding was not clearly spelled out. Still, the cultural agreement resulted in the establishment of a Japan culture center in Berlin, and of a German culture center in Tokyo. These centers typically contained vernacular-language libraries and sponsored art exhibits, musical performances, public lectures, and cinema showings. There were parallel activities between Japan and Italy. The Japanese, moreover, were interested in developing similar programs elsewhere. A Japanese culture center was established in New York in 1938 under KBS auspices. Headed by Maeda Tamon, a former official of the International Labor Organization, the center sponsored lectures on Japanese society and culture, conducted language lessons, and circulated books in U.S. libraries.

By the end of the 1930s, there were probably more officially promoted cultural activities in Japan than ever, and the theme of culture came to play a central role in governmental policy. In 1937, for example, the government initiated a system of awarding annual "culture medals" to those who were considered to have made the greatest contribution in the fields of the sciences, the humanities, the arts, or literature. The authorities clearly wanted to distinguish these awards from military medals or titles of the nobility, as if to show to the rest of the world that the country still valued cultural achievements, whatever the military were engaged in doing in China and elsewhere. In a similar vein, in 1939 a Japanese Foreign Ministry official asserted that, whereas political relations among nations would undergo change from time to time, their cultural connections were more enduring: Japan, he said, must identify with the global trend toward deeper and deeper intercultural relations. That was the only way for the nation to avoid cultural isolation.[50] Also in 1939, after a cultural exchange agreement was signed between Japan and Italy, a Tokyo official asserted that cultural exchange was not subordinate to political affairs; on the contrary, close cultural ties would produce political connections.[51] This was the language of the 1920s adapted to the 1930s, and it indicated that the economic, political, and military crises of the latter decade were forcing governments to pay even greater attention to cultural issues than ever before.

Examples can be multiplied. They all indicate that culture and politics were coming closer together. Put another way, culture, by being officially sponsored and promoted, was becoming politicized. This had been true in a broad sense in the 1920s, but the connection was being made more explicit in the

1930s. To continue with a few more Japanese examples, Ishihara Kanji, one of the architects of Japan's continental imperialism, consistently argued that "human culture and nature" were inexorably leading to a situation where East and West would confront each other for a final showdown. Japan represented the former, and the United States the latter, so war between the two Pacific powers was inevitable. Whichever side won the conflict would have the historic task of reuniting humanity, amalgamating Eastern and Western civilizations. The golden age of peace would then arrive. In Ishihara's view, Japan had to be the victor because it already possessed characteristics derived from the world's major civilizations. The nation had the historic mission of creating "mankind's final and highest civilization."[52]

Ishihara was unique in pushing the cultural argument to its logical conclusion and making that the basis of a predicted war with the United States, but he was by no means alone in stressing the cultural significance of Japanese strategy, wars, and war preparedness in the 1930s. In a well-known guide to schoolteachers published in 1937, *Kokutai no hongi* (The essences of the nation), the Japanese Ministry of Education asserted that Japan's unique martial spirit was the spirit of harmony and, therefore, that when the nation fought in defence of its culture, it did so, not for destruction, oppression, or conquest, but for creation and peace.[53] Uda Hisashi, an influential spokesman for official policy, termed the war against China "a holy war" for "the protection, promotion, and creation of a superior culture that promises mankind's just progress."[54] According to a right-wing professor at the Tokyo Imperial University, neither war nor peace was an end in itself; both were for "life," which meant "the nation's spiritual existence and cultural tradition." "Constant creation and development of culture" was the ultimate objective of all human activities, which was possible only through some kind of spiritual tension. Even death in battle was a religious experience for obtaining "the great harmony of life."[55]

Such extreme statements were by no means limited to Japan. In Germany, which inspired Japanese thought on national and international affairs in this period more than any other country, similar expressions could be found, to indicate the politicization of culture. The idea of German (*Volk*) culture as a unifying theme for the Nazi nation by definition implied that this was the representation of all Germans, past, present, and future, but rejected all aliens and outsiders. There could be no such thing as an internationalized or internationalizable culture, which was a contradiction in terms. "There is no place for a man," one German writer asserted, "where he may exist as a nonpolitical being, in which he could be dispensed from fighting. . . . Human existence is in itself political."[56] According to Carl Schmitt, one of the more prolific and sophisticated writers in Nazi Germany, politics had lost its meaning in the liberal, constitutional, and utilitarian setting of the 1920s, but now the Nazis were restoring it to its rightful place. "A universal organization in which there is no place for warlike preservation and destruction of human existence, would be neither a State nor an Empire; it would lose all political character."[57]

Cultural activities, too, had to be endowed with "political character"; that is, founded upon national essences. The very politicization of culture, however, could allow for the study of other cultures. It is interesting to note that during the 1930s professorships of Japanese studies were established in Vienna and Munich (such positions had earlier existed only in Hamburg and Leipzig), and that the new journal, *Berlin-Rome-Tokyo*, was launched in 1939 "to deepen international relations of all people of the Axis powers." Because Nazi racism left no room for a racial justification for the Axis pact, Germans stressed the superior qualities of Japanese culture in explaining to themselves reasons for an alliance with an Asian nation.[58]

How about the democracies? In the early years of the 1930s, there was much confusion as to what vocabulary was relevant in a situation buffeted by economic and social turmoil. Words and terms popular in the 1920s had become "vacuous"—so wrote Nathaniel Peffer, a Columbia University political scientist, in 1934. That same year, the popular writer George Boas wrote, "One notices a certain shame among liberals and democrats of today, as if they dared not avow their beliefs. They act like pariahs, satisfied to be allowed to vegetate."[59] Those who refused to vegetate, however, began groping for ways to bridge the gap that, they thought, had existed between U.S. culture and U.S. politics. As Richard Pells has suggested, liberal and radical intellectuals were prone to consider the ills of a Depression-driven society fundamentally cultural, believing that the country was in need of a cultural revolution if it were to overcome the economic crisis.[60] The capitalist stress on acquisitiveness, selfishness, and materialism would have to be replaced by an alternative way of life, a new philosophy. Although there was no easy consensus as to what the new philosophy might be, most were agreed that the cultural transformation required political action, which in turn raised the question of power. Thus it would not be enough merely to talk of reform and to engage in cultural activities apart from national political affairs.

Reminiscing about those days, Malcolm Cowley, then a re-
porter for the *New Republic,* has written that, whereas in the
1920s artists and writers in the United States had focused on
"the bright inner world" that had appeared to hold more ex-
citing prospects for creative endeavors than the drab existen-
tial world, now they were discovering that it was "the outer
world" that demanded "to be imaginatively portrayed."[61]
Artists, literary figures, and intellectuals were becoming aware
of the political implications of their activities; that whatever
they did conveyed a message that went beyond purely artistic
or intellectual pursuits and implied a political agenda. Culture
and power were seen to be mutually dependent, not mutually
antagonistic, because it was becoming more and more apparent that in order to preserve American culture ("our way of
life"), it might be necessary to use force.[62]

The title of Reinhold Niebuhr's influential *Christianity and
Power Politics,* published just after the outbreak of World War
II, summed up the emerging thought; culture and politics had
to reinforce each other. As the theologian wrote, to do nothing in the face of the fascist challenge abroad was itself a political act, indicating an indifference to the preservation of the
basic values for which the democratic peoples stood. They
must have enough confidence in themselves to want to fight
totalitarianism. "Whatever may be the moral ambiguities of
the so-called democratic nations, and however serious may be
their failure to conform perfectly to their democratic ideals, it
is sheer moral perversity to equate the inconsistencies of a democratic civilization with the brutalities which modern tyranni-
cal States practice."[63]

If the connection between culture and politics was thus
being stressed not just in totalitarian but also in democratic

states, would this not lead to the obliteration of differences between these two sets of nations? Even more seriously, if the democracies were to defend their culture by force, and Germans and Japanese their respective cultures, also by military power, would this not result in national cultural essentialisms, with little possibility for international communication? For cultural internationalists, this was as serious a challenge in the 1930s as the rise of fascist cultures. Aldous Huxley, for instance, insisted, "'Defending democracy' . . . sounds fine; but to defend democracy by military means, one must be militarily effective, and one cannot become militarily effective without centralising power, setting up a tyranny, imposing some form of conscription or slavery to the state. In other words, the military defence of democracy in contemporary circumstances entails the abolition of democracy even before war starts."

What Huxley was saying, in our context, was that once culture embraced power to preserve itself, it would inevitably alter its character and lose its autonomy. As he argued, "The worst way of dealing with one evil is to do another evil, or to threaten another evil." Whatever cultural values a country had would be lost in preparing for and waging war, because armed conflict tended to obliterate national distinctions; "the results of war are always identical . . . people are slaughtered and a passionate sense of wrong and desire for vengeance are created in the survivors—feelings which make yet further wars inevitable."[64] Robert Aron, a prominent French commentator on current affairs, was in essential agreement with such views when he defended the Munich agreement of 1938—an agreement that, he wrote, gave France an opportunity "to build a new program of peace and European civilization." Germany under Hitler faced two choices, war or peace, and "it depended on us whether he [Hitler] would orient himself toward one or the other." Through the Munich accord, Europe could once again be an arena for the flourishing of civilization. That was France's "mission civilisatrice."[65]

The only effective way to combat such argument was to assert, more strongly than ever, the essential distinction between totalitarian and democratic cultures. As Niebuhr wrote, if one could not make a distinction between democracy and tyranny, "there are no historical distinctions which have any value. All the distinctions upon which the fate of civilization has turned in the history of mankind have been just such relative distinctions."[66] Norman Angell agreed, writing in 1939, as the war came, "[The] principle on behalf of which Britain and France have declared war is in truth the fundamental principle of all organised society and of orderly civilisation. . . . The principle they now defend is the basis, not merely of social, political and economic security, but the necessary condition of those activities which give value to life; which the eighteenth-century Enlightenment defined as the Rights of Man, and we had too readily assumed had been conquered, in the West at least, for all time." Like Niebuhr, Angell, one of the foremost internationalist writers of the first decades of the twentieth century, asserted, "If in the midst of war's appalling agonies we get the feeling that despite the rhetoric it will not make much difference in the long run whether we or the enemy is victorious, the feeling that both will be engulfed in a common ruin anyhow. . . if that feeling gain possession of us, then we shall have lost this war."[67]

Whether such a reaffirmation of cultural differences would, once the war ended, produce a workable solution to the problem of reconstructing internationalism remained to be seen.

Much depended on the activities by the cultural internationalists who had sought to keep alive their vision even in the darkest moments of the 1930s and who would continue to do so during the war. In the meantime, the title of Angell's book *For What Do We Fight?* suggested, not simply that culture was an integral part as much of war making as of peacemaking, but also that, in the peace to come, cultural foundations would once again be considered a critical factor. It was as if the displacement of an earlier cultural internationalism by the growing politicization of culture had never obliterated the need for cultural underpinnings of national and international affairs. Culture, in other words, retained its centrality. That was one of the most important ways in which the world of the 1930s was connected to that of the 1920s.

As if to ridicule the sociologist Robert Park's assertion, in 1926, that "races and cultures die . . . but civilization lives on," the 1930s saw self-conscious races and self-centered cultures combine themselves with national power in Europe and Asia to challenge the assumption of the 1920s that as civilization spread there would emerge a stronger cosmopolitan consciousness. Cultures became more than ever firmly embedded in national frameworks. The situation boded ill for cultural internationalism. And yet Germany, the Soviet Union, Japan, the United States, and other countries, each in its own way, promoted cultural relations with other countries. Few of these activities were in the same spirit of cultural internationalism that had been manifest earlier, but ultimately this spirit was to be reinvoked as the democracies went to war in defence of certain universal values.

CHAPTER FOUR

The Cultural Foundations of the New Globalism

The future of cultural internationalism, and indeed of the human race, hung in a balance when war came in 1939, enveloping most countries of the world. Not just in totalitarian states but in the democracies, the vogue for geopolitical thinking, a necessary precondition for military victory, threatened to extinguish what remained of cultural internationalist forces. Nevertheless, these forces proved resilient and were reincorporated into the postwar world order.

The world after World War II differed, however, from the one before in many significant respects and presented novel challenges to cultural internationalism, most notably in the shape of the cold war and the phenomenon known as the rise of the Third World. In one chapter of this brief book it will be impossible to trace the history of post-1945 cultural internationalism systematically; rather, some examples will be cited to show how cultural internationalism asserted, adapted, and modified itself to meet these challenges.

The global conflict of 1939–45 buffeted cultural internationalism in three ways. First, and most obviously, the war inevitably nationalized cultural pursuits, which came to be seen as part of the total military effort. Second, the world war was accompanied by worldwide revolution: everywhere, and particularly in colonial and underdeveloped areas, profound social turmoil was ensuring that there would be no simple return to the pre-1939 world. Third, national and international security would certainly emerge as the overriding preoccupation of the victorious powers. If cultural internationalism were to survive, it was imperative for its exponents, even during the war, to try to come to terms with these phenomena.

"This has been from the start a war of ideas as well as of men and machines," Max Lerner wrote in August 1941.[1] The words sounded almost trite by then, for it was clearly recognized that the war had cultural as well as geopolitical dimensions; that the two were essentially inseparable. The cultural underpinnings of the war effort were stressed by the anthropologist Margaret Mead in her popular book published shortly after Pearl Harbor, *And Keep Your Powder Dry* (1942). Mead noted that North Americans, British, and other democratic peoples were fighting for their culture. Their war would be different from the war the Germans and Japanese were fighting. Just as Americans were products of their culture, so were the Japanese of theirs and the Germans of theirs; and the war was pitting one cultural definition against another. There was such a thing as a democratic way of war, a democratic victory also, that would strengthen the cultural traditions of the democratic states. But to achieve this end the democracies must militarily crush the Axis powers, which were driven by their own cultural agendas. Put this way, culture as a way of life provided the basic rationale for the war; each country was fighting for its culture. In such fashion, Germans and Japanese, no less than Americans and British, constructed their war.

It is not surprising that cultural themes became particularly pronounced when the Asian war and the European war were combined into one in December 1941, following Japan's attack on U.S. territory and European possessions in the Pacific. Americans and Japanese in particular became more than ever conscious of their different behavior patterns, not to mention their racial distinctions. As John Dower has skillfully demonstrated in *War without Mercy* (1985), the two peoples viewed each other as representatives of diametrically opposed ways of life and thought, in some extreme moments even believing they belonged to different species. Such excesses aside, there is little doubt that the awareness of cultural differences played an important role in wartime perceptions of each other and, even more important, conceptions about the meaning of the war. For the Americans, to be sure, it was a simple matter of avenging themselves for the "sneak attack" on Pearl Harbor, but even such a formulation assumed that there was an essential cultural conflict between the two peoples and that the conflict would not end until one side—obviously, Japan—capitulated completely and mended its ways.

The Japanese, even more than Americans, were conscious of, and fascinated by, the cultural significance of the war. Time and again their leaders reminded the nation that the war against China (which, as seen in chapter 3, had been given cultural significance) had now become part of a global war between East and West. The Asians had the obligation to rally round Japan's mission to save them from Western domination. In a book published in 1943, Haruyama Yukio, a Japanese poet (and a member of "the association of literary figures serving the nation"—a patriotic organization of writers), noted that just as in Europe efforts were being made to reconstruct the foundations of Western culture, in Asia cultural endeavors must lie at the basis of the war. However, unlike Europe, Asian countries generally did not enjoy high standards of living; the task of cultural construction, therefore, must start with agriculture, living conditions, medicine, education, entertainment, and similar areas. This was especially true of Southeast Asia, where, Haruyama argued, the indigenous people's cultural standards were extremely low. Japan's mission lay, therefore, in raising their living standards, through which alone would it become possible to construct an East Asian co-prosperity sphere. Using a dichotomous scheme that had been fashionable in prewar Germany, the author noted that whereas in China the splendid traditional culture had not been matched by a civilization enabling its people to adapt to modern conditions, in the United States a highly developed material civilization had brought about cultural confusion. The new Asia would need both civilization and culture, and here Japanese artists, educators, and intellectuals had an important role to play, because at bottom the Asian war was a war for the creation of a new culture.[2]

The stress on cultural themes was self-serving. Japan was engaged in a war of conquest, and yet the Japanese desperately wanted to believe that their war was different from traditional, Western wars—wars that had aimed at territorial conquest and material benefits. The only plausible way in which the Asian war could be distinguished from Western wars was to argue that Japan was engaged in a new kind of struggle—a struggle for establishing a co-prosperity sphere on the basis of "the spirit of Asian culture," as another writer pointed out. Japan had been too apt to emulate the Western powers' "realism," but now it had parted company with them and was trying to follow "the ideals which were completely Asian." The nation must persuade the fellow Asians, who had also been prone to follow the path of Westernization, to awaken to their Asian destiny and join together in reconstructing "Asian ideology, Asian political organization, and Asian society."[3]

The rhetoric of Asianism was ineffectual. It did not impress Chinese, Filipinos, Indonesians, Burmese, and other Asians who daily experienced Japanese rule and saw little difference between it and the prewar rule by Europeans and North Americans. This can be seen in the fact that in most occupied countries "collaborators" were a small minority; the majority either were indifferent to Asianist propaganda or actively resisted it. It is true that some spoke pan-Asianist language. As late as July 1944, a Burmese scholar was quoted in the Philippine press as saying that the thing that had impressed him most about the Philippines was "the prevailing feeling among the Filipinos that they are Asians bound together by a common background with all other peoples of Asia" and that "the common background of being Asians" united Filipinos and Burmese.[4] Japanese authorities sought to encourage such sentiments by inviting a number of students and intellectuals to Japan. According to historian Grant Goodman, at least some of them shared these sentiments.[5] Nevertheless, the very fact that Japan's cultural propaganda intensified as the tides of war turned against it suggests the futility of the whole campaign and the chasm between rhetoric and reality.

None of this alters the fact that the cultural dimension of the war was taken seriously by the Japanese as well as by the allies. This can be seen, for instance, in the convening in Tokyo, at the end of 1943, of an East Asian conference, bringing together heads of state from Asian countries. True, the countries were occupied by Japanese forces, so the "heads of state" represented little more than collaborators, whether active or passive, but to the Japanese planners for the conference, including Foreign Minister Shigemitsu Mamoru, here was an opportunity to demonstrate to the world Japan's cultural mission: that the nation was engaged in a struggle with the Western powers for control over the destiny of Asian people. Japanese officials echoed the widespread wartime sentiments and incorporated them into a joint declaration issued at the end of the conference. The East Asian Declaration is notable for its stress on culture: the countries of Great East Asia, the declaration asserted, "will respect their respective traditions, promote each people's creativity, and enhance the culture of the whole East Asia." Furthermore, they "will maintain friendly relations with all nations, abolish systems of racial discrimination, undertake extensive cultural exchanges, voluntarily open up their resources, and thus contribute to the progress of the entire world."[6]

It is easy to dismiss such a declaration as nothing but empty rhetoric, but the document contains a clue to the understanding of the wartime role of culture: the drafters of the declaration consciously patterned it after the Atlantic Charter, issued by President Franklin D. Roosevelt and Prime Minister Winston Churchill at the conclusion of their meeting off the coast of Nova Scotia in August 1941. The Atlantic Charter was clearly intended as a statement of differences between their cause and that of their adversaries, and the Japanese felt the need to respond in kind, with their own cultural propaganda.

It is interesting that the Atlantic Charter said nothing directly about cultural preservation and exchange; in this, the Tokyo statement was different. But this should not be taken as indicative of Washington's and London's indifference to the theme; on the contrary, the Atlantic Charter was a cultural document in that it envisioned a postwar world of freedom, justice, and interdependence in which people everywhere would enjoy security and social welfare. It is noteworthy that, in comparison with the Fourteen Points that had spelled out the objectives of the United States during World War I, the Atlantic Charter laid stress on economic and social security as a prerequisite for a durable peace. In other words, the postwar world was visualized not simply in terms of power (the defeat of the Axis) and economics (freedom to engage in productive activities without restriction), but also of culture, broadly defined. To lay stress on decent standards of living, job security, and social welfare as a condition for peace was to conceptualize a connection between domestic and international affairs even more explicitly than earlier. Going beyond the Wilsonian formulation of a stable international order built on democratic governments, the U.S. and British leaders were developing a vision of global interdependence on the basis of shared concerns for security, welfare, and decency. As a British commentator, David Mitrany, noted in 1943, the "universal pressure for social reform" was transforming "the relation of nationalism to internationalism." The task the war was bequeathing to the postwar world, then, was to organize international affairs in such a way that, while the independence of nations was protected, social forces transcending existing political boundaries could somehow be accommodated and served.[7]

That vision would be broadly cultural. But this very broadening of the definition of culture was a serious challenge—the second major issue confronted by cultural internationalists as they looked to the end of the war. They recognized that the war was giving rise to revolutionary changes throughout the world. Not simply in the belligerent countries but throughout the globe rapid changes required a reformulation of internationalism.

A good example of such thinking was in E. H. Carr's influential book, *Conditions of Peace,* published in 1944. Just before the outbreak of the war, Carr had written the well-known critique of interwar internationalism, *Twenty Years' Crisis* (1939). It contained a scathing attack on the ideas of international cooperation as exemplified by the League of Nations. Although he had not commented specifically on the League's activities in the sphere of intellectual cooperation, this was implied in Carr's overall assault on what he considered to be naïveté—a naïveté that, he wrote, had been characteristic of British (and by implication, other democracies') foreign policy. The 1939 book was a plea for realism—for going back to traditional power politics as the starting point for a sensible basis on which to construct a peaceful international system. In the 1944 book, however, Carr argued that the postwar world would not be tenable so long as the nations of the world held on to the balance-of-power approach. "Neither security nor peace," he wrote, "can properly be made the objective of policy," for these concepts had tended to be developed in isolation from domestic social conditions. But the developments during the 1930s, in Germany and the Soviet Union as well as in the democracies, had clearly revealed that forces for social change had become pervasive, and no peace would work unless it came to terms with them. To ignore the upheavals and movements for change or to try to deal with them merely in a rigid framework of international affairs would be counterproductive. The postwar world order must be built on the premise that profound social, economic, and political changes were going to continue everywhere. In such a situation, stability as a goal must be replaced by a commitment to "revolutionise"; international affairs, as much as domestic issues, must be "approached with the desire not to stabilise, but to revolutionise."[8]

Interestingly, to recognize revolutionary social changes as the starting point for constructing the postwar world implied a renewed commitment to internationalism, because it was quite obvious that those changes could not be dealt with merely within the framework of individual nations. Moreover, in many parts of the globe, new states were in the throes of being established. The war was destabilizing the colonial empires, and everywhere, from Morocco to India, from Indochina to Indonesia, nationalistic forces were being unleashed, making unlikely an orderly return to the prewar status quo. As Wendell Willkie, a former Republican presidential candidate, asserted in his *One World* (1942), aspirations for freedom and independence had grown stronger than ever during the war, and the United States and its allies had to identify with those aspirations, or they would lose the initiative in shaping the world after the war. But here again, as the title of Willkie's book showed, the problem of colonial autonomy would have to be dealt with in an international framework, for all movements for freedom and independence were closely linked and required what the *New Republic* called, as early as 1941, "positive international cooperation in the economic and social fields."[9]

As if to respond to such a plea, the victorious nations, which by the spring of 1945 had come to count more than fifty, established an economic and social committee as an important part of the postwar world organization, the United Nations. At the Dumbarton Oaks conference, held in 1944 to plan for

the establishment of a postwar world organization, the delegates from the United States, Britain, the Soviet Union, and
China focused on the security question. (They were to be
made permanent members of the Security Council, with veto
power, an innovation that had not existed in the League.) The
four big powers worked out an arrangement whereby they
would serve as, in essence, global policemen. Interestingly
enough, this arrangement was challenged when a larger international conference was convened, in San Francisco in April
1945, formally to launch the United Nations Organization.
There representatives from other countries were adamant in
insisting on the importance of going beyond narrowly defined
conceptions of security if the peace were to be made durable
after the defeat of the Axis aggressors. Not just military and
geopolitical arrangements, so as to keep the former enemies in
check, but measures to promote economic development and
well-being of all countries would be required. The plea was incorporated into the preamble of the U.N. charter, which declared that the "peoples of the world" were determined to
"promote social progress and better standards of life in larger
freedom" and to "employ international machinery for the promotion of the economic and social advancement of all people." To realize such goals, an Economic and Social Council
was organized as an integral part of the U.N. body, to concern
itself with "international social, economic, cultural, educational, health, and related matters" and "human rights and
fundamental freedoms for all."[10]

It should be noted that in this document cultural matters
were combined with social and economic issues, reflecting the
belief that now, more than ever, these problems were inter-
connected; that postwar internationalism needed to be much

more broadly conceptualized than earlier. Cultural internationalists well understood this. As Alfred Zimmern, one of the
most devoted disciples of this movement in the interwar years,
noted in a thoughtful memorandum he wrote shortly after the
war, "If the League of Nations Organization of Intellectual
Cooperation did not fulfil all the hopes of its founders, this
was not so much because it failed in the tasks that it undertook
as because there had been insufficient consideration of the nature of those tasks. . . . Membership of . . . an organisation dedicated to the things of the mind, carries with it a constant
obligation to keep the reality of interdependence in the fore-
front of the consciousness." That would mean that postwar
cultural internationalism must take the "diversity of cultures"
seriously, not assuming an air of superiority over the remote
and the unfamiliar. Moreover, ordinary people in all lands
must come within its purview. Why was it, Zimmern asked,
"that during the period when the League of Nations Commission of Intellectual Cooperation was holding its annual
meetings the cause of intellectual freedom . . . suffered a set-
back such as had not been experienced in the West for many
centuries?" The answer was simple: the organization was oc-
cupying itself "with the tools of the intellectual and artistic life
rather than with the nature of that life itself."[11]

While Zimmern, and others, thus argued for broadening
the scope of cultural internationalism, they were also intent on
establishing a world organization charged especially with promoting cultural projects, rather than having these projects undertaken within the Economic and Social Council. Those who
had been active in the League's intellectual cooperation activities never let up their efforts, even during the war, determined
to resurrect the movement as soon as peace returned.

It was noted in chapter 3 how one prominent cultural internationalist, Henri Bonnet, occupied himself energetically with the task in the United States, to which he came in 1941 after fleeing from France. Eager to continue the work begun so promisingly at the Paris Institute for Intellectual Cooperation, Bonnet kept in close touch with James Shotwell and other U.S. internationalists. When, for instance, intellectual leaders from the United States and other American states met in Havana in November 1941 to hold a colloquium on "the intellectual life of America and its relationship to universal culture," Bonnet was there to seek to interest the delegates in continuing the projects of the institute.[12] When he remained in the United States after the liberation of France, to serve as Charles de Gaulle's ambassador in Washington, others took over the task of reopening the Paris institute. As soon as it was reopened, in the early months of 1945, the institute resumed some of its prewar activities, and its leaders hoped it would in time become the key organization working with the United Nations to promote cultural internationalism. Others, however, believed a new institution was needed that would be broader in scope and more representative of the whole world.

It is interesting to note that at the San Francisco conference in the spring of 1945 that led to the founding of the United Nations, many delegates talked of the need for "educational and cultural cooperation," not just "intellectual cooperation," as prewar internationalists had been wont to do.[13] The stress on education reflected the concern in the allied capitals with the rebuilding of war-devastated schools and libraries so as to prepare the younger generation for the task of peace-building. Such a concern was reflected, for instance, in a U.S. Congressional resolution introduced in early 1945 by Senators J. William Fulbright and Robert Taft for the establishment of an international office of education. It seemed clear to them, and to many of their colleagues who supported the initiative, that educational reconstruction was one of the vital necessities in the postwar world and that only a world agency, not national bodies, could cope with the challenge.

Even more impressive was the fact that, throughout the war, the allied ministers of education had met in London to consider "educational and cultural reconstruction" after the war. These gatherings were one of the least-known episodes of World War II. It is impressive that they were started in 1942, in the middle of incessant bombings of London, in makeshift quarters. They brought together officials and educators from many allied nations, some of which had been occupied by the Axis and were functioning through governments in exile in Britain.[14] Initially consisting of European officials, in time they were joined by delegates from the United States, China, and other countries. At first they were concerned with helping school teachers and pupils in occupied areas and considered ways of sending books and supplies to them. Soon their objectives were broadened and, as the war neared its end, the ministers of education became eager to consider a more formal structure—an international organization for resuming cultural cooperation and educational exchange after the war.

Their thinking may be seen in work done throughout 1944 and 1945 on a preamble for such an organization. As amended by the U.S. State Department in August 1944, the draft read in part:

The cold blooded and considered destruction by the fascist governments of the cultural resources of great parts of the continents of Europe and Asia; the murder of teachers, artists, scientists and intellectual leaders; the burning of books; the pillaging and mutilation of works of art; the rifling of archives and the theft of scientific apparatus, have created conditions dangerous to civilization, and therefore to peace. . . . To deprive any part of the interdependent modern world of the cultural resources, human and material, through which its children are trained and its people informed, is to destroy to that extent the common knowledge and the mutual understanding upon which the peace of the world and its security must rest.[15]

The statement indicated that the spirit of the cultural internationalism of the interwar years had not been destroyed by the horrible experiences of World War II; on the contrary, it had been reaffirmed. As in the 1920s, there was strong determination to reconstruct the international system on cultural foundations. At the same time, the connection between international peace and security, on the one hand, and cultural understanding, on the other, needed to be spelled out more clearly than before, because it could be, and was, argued that interwar cultural internationalism had done little or nothing to prevent war, and that its advocates had been totally wrong in ignoring the power realities in international relations. This, the connection between cultural internationalism and international security, was the third challenge faced by the movement's advocates.

Perhaps the best-known exponent of the "realist" critique of cultural internationalism was Nicholas Spykman, a Dutch-born journalist/scholar teaching at Yale University, whose book *America's Strategy in World Politics* (1942) was enormously influential (as well as controversial). Spykman's main aim was to stress geopolitics and balance of power as principal factors in international relations. The book contained scathing attacks on what he called the "naive idea that, in a world of power politics, states co-operate because their populations admire each other." Criticizing efforts at what he called "cultural rapprochement" between the United States and the Latin American republics, Spykman sarcastically noted, "If the cooperation of our Latin neighbors is dependent on the popular appreciation of the rhumba in the United States, the future is indeed bright."

From a political point of view, Spykman asserted that a "program of cultural rapprochement" was "the most useless form of ideological warfare, whatever may be its value as a program of adult education."[16] Cultural internationalists could argue back, saying it was precisely adult education, not ideological warfare, that would lay the groundwork for the postwar world order, but they still had to reckon with the fact that the Axis powers' assault on the international community had given rise to the vogue of geopolitical realism of the kind represented by Spykman's writings.

As was the case elsewhere, however, the realist revival served not to destroy but to revitalize cultural internationalism. It was promoted not as an alternative to military and security considerations but as constituting, along with these considerations, a vital part of the new agenda for peace. The draft preamble quoted above was a good example. As it further asserted, "Cooperative activity in education and in the furtherance of cultural interchange among the peoples of the world will promote the freedom, the dignity, and the wellbeing of all, and therefore assist in the attainment of security and peace." The proposed organization for educational and cultural exchange, the statement continued, was designed "to repair . . . the injury done to the common cultural inheritance of the world by the fascist powers, and to lay the foundation of the establishment . . . of a continuing international organization dedicated to the proposition that the free and unrestricted education of the peoples of the world, and the free and unrestricted interchange between them of ideas and knowledge, are essential to the preservation of security and peace."

Such a statement indicates that visions of postwar international relations solidly grounded on cultural communication were strongly reaffirmed, and that they were now strengthened by an incorporation into them of broad social and security concerns. The internationalists were willing to accept that social and security considerations would have to play a more pivotal role in the new world order, but at the same time they insisted that cultural underpinnings be given even to "security and peace." Just as social and economic factors were now brought into focus through the establishment of the Economic and Social Council of the United Nations, cultural internationalism was codified in the Educational, Scientific, and Cultural Organization (UNESCO).

UNESCO was essentially a continuation of the prewar Committee on Intellectual Cooperation, but as the new organization's title indicates, it was conceived more broadly. The inclusion of education in the agenda for cross-national cooperation was a direct outcome of the deliberations of the allied ministers of education during the war. Scientific undertakings were incorporated into the agreement toward the end of the war as officials, especially from the United States, argued the need for internationalizing scientific research. In a way the war had already realized this objective, most notably in atomic physics, but it was hoped that in other fields, too, scientists would continue to work together within the framework of postwar internationalism.

UNESCO was even more representative of non-Western

countries than its predecessor. The International Committee on Intellectual Cooperation, as noted above, had already been notable because its members came from all regions of the globe, but the intellectual leadership had tended to lie in European and North American hands. UNESCO, reflecting the diverse membership in the United Nations, was destined to become an arena for initiatives as much from Asia, Africa, the Middle East, and Latin America as from Europe and North America.

The UNESCO constitution, completed in London in November 1945, categorically declared that "since wars begin in the minds of men, it is in the minds of men that the defences of peace must be constructed." Indeed, the language of the constitution's preamble echoed exactly the rhetoric of prewar cultural internationalism:

The wide diffusion of culture, and the education of humanity for justice and liberty and peace are indispensable to the dignity of man and constitute a sacred duty which all the nations must fulfill in a spirit of mutual assistance and concern; . . . a peace based exclusively upon the political and economic arguments of governments would not be a peace which could secure the unanimous, lasting and sincere support of the peoples of the world, and . . . the peace must therefore be founded . . . upon the intellectual and moral solidarity of mankind.

Even more than its parental body, the United Nations, UNESCO was seen as a universal, inclusive organization. In the wake of so much race hatred, genocide, and mass destruction, there was determination to strengthen internationalism through an unambiguous assertion of national, ethnic, and racial equality as the basis for undertaking the tasks of cultural communication. A Cuban delegate at the preparatory commission for establishing UNESCO observed that its primary aim ought to be "action which benefits the greatest number [touching] the lives and welfare of the masses of men and women in all lands."[17] He went on to suggest that one of the first tasks of UNESCO should be the reduction of inequalities in educational and cultural opportunities within each nation and among the member states comprising the United Nations. These and many similar expressions by those on the preparatory commission—they came from China, Cuba, Mexico, South Africa, the United States, and several European countries—indicated the shared belief that the new internationalism would be an even more ambitious proposition, inviting the participation of all countries to combat "the doctrine of the inequality of men and races," as the UNESCO constitution asserted.

The UNESCO declaration on human rights, issued with a fanfare in 1948, was a ringing reendorsement of cultural internationalism, now considerably broadened. Asserting that "a world in which human beings shall enjoy freedom of speech and belief and freedom from fear and want" represented "the highest aspirations of the common people," the declaration defined itself as "a common standard of achievement for all peoples and all nations," so that they would promote, through teaching and education, respect for these rights and freedoms.

With its national branches (commissions) throughout the world, UNESCO was set to engage in many activities, ranging from the collaborative writing of a cultural history of the world to the preservation of ancient artistic monuments, projects that were reminiscent of those of the interwar years but that were now more global in scale. (It is a remarkable fact that already at a 1947 meeting of UNESCO in Mexico City, the participants voted to extend its activities to Japan. Japanese observers were invited to attend the 1950 gathering of the organization held in Florence, and in June 1951—with three months still to go before the San Francisco peace conference that put an end to the U.S. occupation of the country—Japan was formally invited to join UNESCO. Japanese political and intellectual leaders took this membership extremely seriously and were soon participating in a number of colloquia and engaging in several collaborative research projects. In 1956, when the ninth plenary meeting of UNESCO was convened in New Delhi, Japanese delegates were instrumental in having their colleagues from other countries adopt the theme of "mutual understanding between Eastern and Western cultures and values" as a principal project to be undertaken by the organization.)

To what extent UNESCO and other agencies for cultural internationalism have succeeded in imposing a cultural definition of international relations is a key question of post-1945 history. Certainly, it might have seemed, in the wake of the defeat of the Axis powers, that the movement would be pushed with great vigor and contribute to reshaping the world order. In reality, however, it had soon to confront other definitions of world affairs, of which the cold war was the most prominent but by no means the only example.

In this brief survey of cultural internationalism, it is impossible to trace in detail the often tortured evolution of that movement since World War II. That cultural internationalism has been a powerful force in contemporary history cannot be contested, however. To be sure, any generalization about the recent past has to be of necessity tentative, for the generalizer is very much part of the phenomena being described. We lack sufficient distance and perspective to assess the forces that have shaped today's world. "Nobody can write the history of the twentieth century," Eric Hobsbawm has noted in the preface to his *The Age of Extremes: A History of the World, 1914–1991* (1994), "like that of any other era, if only because nobody can write about his or her lifetime as one can (and must) write about a period known only from outside, at second- or third-hand, from sources of the period or the works of later historians."[18] Such caution applies particularly to the study of the second half of the twentieth century, a period that coincides with the lifetimes of most writers and readers today.

Yet even to make such an acknowledgment of a historian's limits is a typically contemporary phenomenon, when it is generally assumed that one has to be self-conscious of one's personal background, ideology, and even politics before undertaking any study. And this self-consciousness is a product, indirect if not direct, of the accumulated sensitivities as a result of cultural dialogues across national boundaries. Moreover, the very fact that Hobsbawm's history of the twentieth century is "a history of the world," devoting considerable space to political and cultural developments in non-Western countries, is evidence that a cultural internationalist perspective is now the common ground on which most scholarly work is carried out.

Nevertheless, it is difficult to deny that the cultural internationalist visions as expressed in UNESCO's declarations have not been fulfilled, and that they have encountered enormous obstacles and challenges. Nationalistic suspicion and resentment of internationalism have remained potent. As John Bodnar has noted in *Remaking America* (1992), in the United States the nation's political, business, and community leaders have actively sought to reaffirm "public memory" through parades, pageants, and monuments to inculcate patriotism, and the same phenomenon undoubtedly exists in most countries.

But the tension between nation-states and internationalist forces is nothing new. What distinguishes the post-1945 period has been the existence of other entities—supranational alliances, regional organizations, subnational "cultures"—that have posed as serious challenges to cultural internationalism as nationalism. To simplify this complex story, it may be useful to consider how two key developments of postwar history, the cold war and the emergence of the Third World, have affected cultural internationalist agendas.

The ideal of cross-national cultural communication and understanding, of course, was compromised by the geopolitical realities of the cold war, as the United States and the Soviet Union waged what has been called World War III on all fronts. Cultural activities, ranging from intelligence gathering and propaganda in the media to student exchanges and subsidies to foreign intellectuals, became instruments of official policy. International power relations defined, to that extent, international cultural relations.

Whether, in these circumstances, there could be such a thing as open cultural exchanges, as envisaged by UNESCO, was a serious question in the early postwar years. If cultural activities were to be undertaken primarily in the geopolitical milieu of the cold war, the future of internationalism would be endangered, and for this very reason, dedicated internationalists sought to keep alive the spirit of cultural interchange. F. O. Matthiessen, the Harvard literary critic and a founder of the Salzburg American seminar, bringing together U.S. and European scholars and students for a summer of intensive conversations—surely an excellent example of cultural internationalism right after the war—insisted in 1947, "the chief function of culture and humanism" was "to bring man . . . into communication with man." In the aftermath of the devastating war and at the beginning of another world crisis, Matthiessen was convinced that only such contact would ensure durable peace and freedom. Contact led to mingling ("the only solid basis" for international order) and to cross-national perspective, away from chauvinism and military confrontation. As he reiterated in 1949, "By perceiving what [one's] country is and is not in comparison with other countries, [one] can help contribute, in this time of fierce national tensions, to the international understanding without which civilization will not survive."[19]

Similarly, in a book published in 1950, *War and Human Progress,* the economist John U. Nef noted that the "seriousness of wars can be mitigated . . . only by the growth of a common community of understanding relating to life as a whole, such as existed to some extent among the peoples of Europe in the age of limited wars during the late seventeenth and much of the eighteenth century." Developments since then, Nef also wrote, had indicated the serious erosion of this community of understanding (a thesis with which one may disagree in view of the internationalist movements traced in these chapters). In any event, Nef went on to say, "This community of understanding can no longer be confined . . . to the Western peoples, for the only community that can preserve Western civilization is a world community, in which both individuals and regions, with their cultures, are given an opportunity to develop their special talents and genius under general law." Such a community, a prerequisite for a stable international order, "should be the work of the human mind and spirit, operating now more than ever independently of politics, of the pomp and circumstance of the states which are engaged in threatening each other."[20]

This was precisely the spirit of postwar cultural internationalism, but unfortunately "the states . . . threatening each other" made it extremely difficult, if not impossible, to develop an international "community of understanding." Instead of Nef's vision, the nightmare of George Orwell's *Nineteen Eighty-Four,* ironically published in the very year (1948) the UNESCO declaration on human rights was issued, seemed to approximate the reality. As if to mock that declaration, Orwell depicted an authoritarian state from which freedom of thought had disappeared and in which historical memory was constantly being reformulated by the people in power. Although more descriptive of Stalinist Russia during the purges than of any nation in the period of the cold war, Orwell's book did point to the difficulties of even conceptualizing a world as a community of nations in free association. In reviewing the book, Lionel Trilling wrote, "The whole effort of the culture of the last hundred years has been directed toward teaching us to understand the economic motive as the irrational road to death." Orwell, Trilling added, was showing that, just as the Soviet system, which was designed presumably to overcome economic ills, had produced a police state, "the social idealism of our democratic culture" might also lead to "the ultimate threat to human freedom" because of the augmentation of political power in the hands of the government. Another reviewer noted that Orwell was saying "there is no hope for man in the political conception of man."[21] (Compare this with the earlier-quoted assertion by Carl Schmitt that there was hope for man only as a political being.) Such pessimistic observations left little room for the pursuit of autonomous cultural activities, let alone cultural internationalism.

Nevertheless, it would be overly simplistic to put postwar

history solely in the framework of the cold war and dismiss all other phenomena, including cultural internationalism, as having been of little, if any, significance. (It is distressing to note that in two recent histories of the twentieth century, both by distinguished scholars, there is not so much as a mention of UNESCO, or of other instances of cultural cooperation after World War II.)[22] Actually, one could argue that cultural internationalist activities were pursued despite—or, in some instances, even because of—the U.S.-Soviet geopolitical confrontation. Cultural internationalism had its own dynamic, as had been the case before the war, and some manifestations of it were only tangentially affected by the cold war. As Maurice Schumann, the French foreign minister, noted in 1970, "There is no area of production, research, speculation, or artistic expressions that does not entail joint projects [among nations] which today constitute a dragnet of nets woven throughout the world."[23]

Some examples of these woven nets will indicate how nations, despite their geopolitical preoccupations, managed, in Schumann's words, to "establish relations of understanding and cooperation" among themselves. In addition to the manifold activities carried out by UNESCO, the parent body itself, the United Nations, actively promoted cultural communication and intellectual cooperation. The fact that the world organization survived many crises brought about by its inability to ensure post-1945 collective security was due to the mushrooming of collaborative endeavors across national boundaries in economic, technical, and cultural spheres. Numerous international committees of experts were set up under the auspices of the Economic and Social Council to report on issues ranging from economic development of underdeveloped areas to scientific cooperation in such areas as atomic energy and space exploration. In December 1953, President Dwight D. Eisenhower proposed, in a speech at the United Nations, international cooperation in the peaceful use of atomic energy. In response, the world organization set up, in 1957 the International Atomic Energy Agency, where experts from various countries would work together, on behalf of the United Nations, to guide nations in the peaceful utilization of nuclear energy. Although space exploration became bound up with the cold war, as the superpowers were eager to develop rockets and satellites in outer space to deliver nuclear weapons, this did not prevent scientists from several countries from undertaking a concerted attempt at regularizing the use of outer space for military purposes. The 1967 "treaty on principles governing the activities of states in the exploration and uses of outer space, including the moon and other celestial bodies" was a direct outcome of this movement. Although none of these agreements would have been achieved if the powers themselves had not supported them, one should recognize them as products of the same spirit of cultural internationalism that had animated prewar scientists.

Likewise, the cold war did not impede postwar exchange programs of students, scholars, and others. In the late 1940s and the 1950s the United States was already hosting hundreds of students from all over the world, including the former enemy countries, the latter under the GARIOA (Government Appropriation for Relief in Occupied Areas) program. In the 1950s, most government-sponsored exchanges were put under the Fulbright program, as good a symbol of postwar cultural internationalism as any. (Some twelve thousand Germans and two thousand Japanese students and scholars visited the

United States through officially sponsored programs during 1947–55, and several hundred more through private funding.) In the meantime, there was a flow of student and scholarly traffic from China and East European countries to the Soviet Union, and from Third World countries to China and the Soviet Union. (More than a thousand Latin American students and intellectuals visited China during the 1950s; in 1962, four thousand officially sponsored Third World students were studying in the Soviet Union.)

Undoubtedly, these phenomena could be seen as a cultural aspect of the cold war, but it would make little sense to connect the "returned students" in many countries to a cold war strategy. They may have been "brainwashed," but this was more an intellectual, and much less a political, phenomenon. Some have argued, for instance, that the social science disciplines learned by foreign students in U.S. colleges and universities in the 1950s were designed to popularize the ideology of liberal capitalism through the concept of modernization. This was undoubtedly the case, but it would be far-fetched to connect it to geopolitical developments. Rather, through educational exchanges, thousands of young men and women were sharing similar intellectual experiences and developing a vocabulary through which they could engage in meaningful interactions. The steady transformation of the cold war from the 1950s to the 1960s, which historians have chronicled, may not have been unrelated to the growth of such interactions.

Some cultural exchange programs developed with their own momentum. For instance, by the 1960s about seven thousand German students were studying in European universities outside Germany, and about eleven thousand students from other European countries in turn were enrolled in German

universities. (Contrast these figures to those in 1910: one hundred German students and six thousand others). Textbook revision, which had been a popular project during the 1920s, was
resumed with renewed vigor. As early as 1950, twenty German
and fifteen French historians met to take up the enterprise and
agreed to hold periodic meetings to evaluate and recommend
revision for their respective national textbooks in history. In
the meantime, in the 1960s UNESCO organized conferences
in the Balkans for representatives of all European countries,
and in 1973 a pan-European meeting of education ministers
took place in Bucharest.24

Perhaps most fascinating in the history of postwar cultural
internationalism is the role of U.S. culture in uniting different
peoples and nations. The phenomenon of Americanization, to
be sure, predated World War II. As noted in chapter 2, during
the 1920s the spread of American culture, especially in con-
sumer goods and popular entertainment, was beginning to
create a global community of shared interests and habits. That
community had never totally disappeared, even during the
more nationalistic decade of the 1930s, as can be seen in the
often virulent reaction against the influx of American movies,
attesting to their continuing popularity. The tragic events of
the war years may have had the effect of further enhancing the
relative position of U.S. cultural influence. As David Hollinger
has shown, the coming of war in Europe persuaded Americans
that the world's cultural, not just geopolitical and economic,
leadership had finally become theirs, with New York likely
to replace Paris as the new center of cosmopolitanism. The
United States, noted Alfred Kazin in 1942, had become "a
repository of Western Culture." In this sense, Reinhold Wagnleitner is undoubtedly correct to argue that Americanization

was built upon Europeanization.[25] The victory over Nazi totalitarianism meant the reaffirmation of European values, and of Western civilization, which now were being reinvigorated and, it seemed, strengthened through the influence of the United States.

Clearly, the trend toward Americanization did not stop at the end of the war but became even more notable in the postwar years, not the least because the U.S. government now actively promoted a cultural policy, not just in the occupied countries—Germany, Austria, Japan—but also in the entire world. Whether or not the forces of cultural Americanization would have taken a different form in the absence of the cold war can be debated endlessly. What seems beyond dispute is that the promotion of American culture predated the coming of the cold war, whether one sees the cold war as starting with the Truman doctrine of 1947, the Korean war of 1950, or some other point. Indeed, as far as Germany, Austria, and Japan were concerned, their Americanization—at least in those areas that came under ·U.S. occupation—was already an accomplished fact by 1947.[26] American cultural influences were no less visible elsewhere, not only where U.S. armed forces remained, such as China and the Philippines, but also in the European colonies in the Middle East and Asia in the throes of revolutionary upheaval. Nationalistic leaders were familiar with U.S. constitutional and political history and often couched their movements in the same vocabulary.

As Elaine Tyler May, Stephen Whitfield, and others have shown, there was a nationalistic aspect to the culture of the United States during the cold war: the nation's education, entertainment, and even family life were often placed in the framework of the imperative to preserve "the American way of

life" against the onslaught of world Communism.[27] Furthermore, during the heyday of McCarthyism, there was skepti-
cism about, if not a rejection of, internationalism. Individuals
and organizations that had been active in international movements such as the Abraham Lincoln Brigade and the Institute
of Pacific Relations came under attack for having allegedly
subordinated national to international interests. Nevertheless,
one should not overlook the fact that, compared with the Soviet Union, the United States remained far more cosmopolitan
even during the height of the cold war. The United States lib-
eralized its immigration policy, admitted a large number of
refugee intellectuals, and invited foreign artists and scholars to
travel freely inside the country. The sense that the United
States was in a position to promote "a creative communion
sweeping across all boundaries," as Harold Rosenberg had put
it in 1940, never disappeared.[28]

In 1941, publisher Henry Luce had asserted that the twentieth century "must be to a significant degree an American
Century." Often taken as an example of nationalistic hubris,
such a statement should be put in the context of the perceived
"one world" that Luce believed to be emerging "for the first
time in history." The implication was clear. The United States
must, Luce said, lead in the task of creating a "world-environ-
ment" that was conducive to peace, justice, and prosperity.
There was, he wrote, already "an immense American internationalism. American jazz, Hollywood movies, American slang,
American machines and patented products, are in fact the only
things that any community in the world . . . recognizes in
common." America, he concluded, "is already the intellectual,
scientific and artistic capital of the world. Americans . . . are
today the least provincial people in the world."[29] However ex-

aggerated, Luce's thesis was as much internationalist as nationalist; indeed, it saw a symbiotic relationship between U.S. nationalism and internationalism. It is fair to say that the phenomena he described in 1941 did not fundamentally change after 1945, and the ultimate end of the cold war and the collapse of Communism were to attest to the salience of his observations. Cultural internationalism in the guise of Americanization, something he was talking about, was destined to survive the geopolitically defined cold war.

At a meeting with congressional leaders held in February 1970, President Richard Nixon said he "eschewed gushy optimism of any kind," adding, "some Americans think that we can rely on peace by sending a few Fulbright scholars abroad . . . but that doesn't bring peace. We can avoid war if we are realistic and not soft-headed."[30] Nixon was reacting to his Democratic predecessors' support of cultural and educational exchange. (In 1961 President John F. Kennedy created the post of assistant secretary of state for educational and cultural affairs, and in 1966 President Lyndon Johnson signed into law the international education act that contained the words "ideas, not armaments, would shape this country's lasting prospects for peace.")[31] Both Kennedy's and Johnson's espousal of cultural diplomacy and Nixon's disdain for it (the latter argued that cultural exchange should be undertaken by private channels) showed that the cold war as such was not an insurmountable obstacle to cultural internationalism.

A potentially more serious challenge arose in the shape of Third Worldism. The emergence of the Third World was a major phenomenon of the post-1945 world, paralleling the U.S.-Soviet confrontation but in many ways even more significant for the discussion of cultural internationalism. If the cold war had a cultural dimension, and if, even during the height of the cold war in the 1950s and the 1960s, cultural Americanization proceeded apace, the rise of the Third World, too, had obvious cultural implications. More than twenty new states were created during 1945–59, and more than thirty during 1959–69. Fifty years after the end of World War II, the world was to consist of more than two hundred independent countries, almost triple the number before the war. The majority of them were in the Third World, and Third World countries were, at least initially, by definition non-European, representing a vast array of ethnic, religious, and linguistic traditions.

We may characterize the Third World as "multicultural" and refer to its self-assertiveness as "multiculturalism." It is at once obvious that the challenges posed by the Third World to postwar cultural internationalism were even more serious than the cold war, which, after all, represented biculturalism in the sense of dividing the world into two ideological camps but in which U.S. cultural influence—a sort of unicultural universalism— proved stronger. How would the Third World respond to these postwar phenomena? That was one of the key issues faced by cultural internationalism.

To be sure, the emergence of the Third World did not in itself constitute a threat to internationalism. UNESCO's declaration on human rights had noted that postwar internationalism, like its prewar definition, included "the right to a nationality." Nationality groups, ancient or recently formed, would cooperate with one another in furtherance of cultural and educational objectives. In that spirit, some of the new nations came together at Bandung, Indonesia, in 1955. The Bandung Conference was the first formal gathering, as a group, of Asian and African countries. The delegates asserted their col-

lective identity in terms of their commitment to nation making and economic development, as well as their adherence to
"five principles of peace" (such as peaceful coexistence and
reciprocity) that, while unexceptional in the Western context,
nevertheless signalled the Third World's determination to stay
as clear as possible of the cold war confrontation between the
superpowers. One of the agreements at the conference was on
cultural exchange. Had this sort of collective action been continued, the Third World might have enriched the vocabulary
and content of cultural internationalism: Asian, African, Middle Eastern, and Latin American nations might have cooperated with one another in the cultural as well as other spheres
and strengthened internationalism, even as it was being undermined by the geopolitics of the cold war.

But the Third World was never united as a community of
nations. It came to split into different segments, and nationalistic rivalries among its members proved as intractable as traditional interstate relations among Western powers. How could
nation-building efforts be reconciled with internationalism?
This was precisely the problem the Western nations had grappled with since the seventeenth century, but the problem was
now even more acute, inasmuch as internationalism historically had been a product of European history.

If, as suggested in chapter 1, nationalism and internationalism had developed in tandem, albeit with a disproportionate
weight on the side of the former, might not the same development take place in the non-Western parts of the world? Could
the newly independent Third World countries also formulate
an internationalist agenda, within or apart from UNESCO
and other world organizations? Must one accept that "every
national movement is a movement for expansion and power"

(as Amos Kenan, the Israeli author and poet, put it)? Kenan argued that "there never has been, nor can there ever be, any alliance between national movements." The only way out of the predicament was "a final peace."[32] But would such a peace not presume a willingness to embrace some internationalist propositions?

Because conflict and tensions became widespread in the Third World, these questions assumed an increased urgency. Were there strong internationalist traditions in non-European countries? For instance, in view of the fact that so many newly independent countries were Islamic, could one say that Islamic internationalism might be a possible force for the new cultural internationalism? What was the relationship between this internationalism and the nationalism of individual countries that embraced Islam? Can it be said, as another author, also Israeli, noted, that the Arab ideology is the "ideology of the usage of force," pitting itself against a set of Israeli values?[33] Similarly, given the emergence of the People's Republic of China as a major power in Asia, to what extent had traditional Confucianism (including the thought of K'ang Yu-wei, mentioned in chapter 1) as well as Maoist Marxism prepared the Chinese people for undertaking internationalist tasks? How did the millions of overseas Chinese, constituting what some have called the Chinese diaspora, contribute to cross-cultural communication?

These questions have remained mostly unexplored, and this is not the place to try such exploration. But until such issues are fully examined, no history of the postwar world will be complete. In our context, it may be noted that Third World countries, both collectively and individually, came to assert themselves in the world arena in proportion as the cold war tensions began to subside. In the 1960s, just as the United

States and the Soviet Union began taking tentative steps toward limiting the nuclear arms race, the Third World became more vociferous, going much beyond the Bandung rhetoric of peaceful coexistence. The membership in the United Nations was now more than half Third World, and its representatives were instrumental in having the world organization call the 1960s "a decade of development," the idea being to call upon the nations to focus on economic issues as a global agenda. But these years also saw serious challenges to the cultural foundations of international relations, as could be seen most graphically when China launched its "great cultural revolution," aimed not only at eradicating the legacies of bourgeois civilization at home but also undermining the cultural and geopolitical influence of the superpowers in Asia, Africa, and elsewhere.

What these phenomena amounted to was a challenge to the assumed universalism of cultural interactions among nations. Modern technological innovations, educational reforms, the spread of mass entertainment, scholarly symposia—all these had seemed to be instruments of cultural internationalism, with mutual understanding and cooperation as the ultimate goal. Increasingly, however, as Third World nations began presenting their own perspectives and agendas, cultural diversity, as well as shared values, came to claim the attention of internationalists.

The situation became even more pronounced in the 1970s, a decade notable on the one hand because of the further relaxation of cold war tensions, and on the other for disarray in the global economic system—this latter phenomenon (exemplified by such drastic events as the "de-coupling" of the dollar from gold and the steep increases in the price of petroleum) putting an end to decades of phenomenal economic growth on the part of the so-called advanced industrial nations. Contemporary observers were talking of "the end of the postwar era." What was equally significant, though few noticed it at first, was the emergence of cultural themes as important keys to international affairs. It was as if the waning of the cold war and the crisis of the world economy were calling forth cultural agendas with greater vigor than ever before, the more so because these agendas now included what came to be known as multicultural perspectives.

To be sure, not all international cultural activities stressed diversity or multiculturalism over universalism. Universal values were ringingly reendorsed at a meeting of the Conference on Security and Cooperation in Europe (CSCE) that took place in Helsinki in 1975. The Soviet Union and other Eastern European countries, as well as the United States and its NATO allies, signed the Helsinki accord, pledging their adherence to the principles of human rights and cultural exchange—items that UNESCO had proclaimed in 1945 and reaffirmed periodically.

As if to suggest that these principles were finally to be applied universally, many governments and private organizations instituted programs for cultural exchange in the 1970s. For instance, exchange programs between countries formally belonging to opposing camps in world politics increased significantly. International scholarly symposia that had for many years been limited to scholars from the United States and its allies began to attract participants from the Soviet Union, China, and elsewhere. As early as 1970, an "international future research conference" was held in Kyoto, marking, according to Kishida Junnosuke, the heralding of the coming of the age of the "third Industrial Revolution."[34] Whether or not one accepts this concept (it refers to revolutionary developments in computer and information technology) it seems clear that these developments, coming just at the time of the relaxation of geopolitical tensions, were facilitating international communication in all scholarly and artistic fields. It is noteworthy, to take just one example—from the rapidly advancing field of biotechnology—that the need for international collaboration was taken for granted: in 1975, the United States Academy of Science organized the first international conference on DNA at Asilomar, California. In the meantime, the establishment of the Committee for Scholarly Cooperation with the People's Republic of China in Washington in the early 1970s had been a sign of the changing environment in which cultural exchanges were fast resuming their importance in the relationship between these two erstwhile cold war antagonists, and the Fulbright program, which had never severed ties to nations in the Soviet bloc, even during the height of the cold war, now sponsored visiting scholars going to Eastern European countries and to China. Joint scientific projects began to be undertaken between nations of the U.S. and Soviet blocs, the U.S.-Soviet cooperative exploration of space in the 1980s being a logical outcome of such a development.

In such an environment, far friendlier to cultural internationalism than the first twenty-five years following World War II, various countries began to earmark larger and larger portions of their funds for programs in educational exchange and intellectual cooperation. Such organizations as the German Marshall Fund, the French-American Foundation, and the Japan Foundation, all established during the 1970s, were semipublic bodies designed to promote cultural projects such as the exchange of visitors, language training, and library support. It is interesting to note that Japanese prime ministers in the 1970s began speaking of promoting mutual understanding as a key objective of the nation's foreign policy: it was as if Japan needed something besides the preservation of security and the expansion of trade as national goals. Prime Minister Takeshita Noboru, in office in the early 1980s, spoke of "three pillars" of Japanese foreign policy: security, economic interests, and cultural exchange. Through the initiative of the Japan Foundation and other organizations, the nation undertook projects ranging from the sending of Kabuki artists and contemporary musicians abroad to the receiving of foreign students for language study. (The number of foreign students in Japan, never more than a couple of thousand before the 1970s, steadily increased and reached twenty thousand by the mid-1980s.) In 1973, a United Nations university was established in Tokyo, with a view to promoting cross-national research into global issues that affected "the survival, development, and welfare of mankind."

One of the first issues taken up by the United Nations University was the protection of the natural environment—an indication that the agendas of cultural internationalism now included issues that had not existed in earlier undertakings. Although alarmist warnings about humankind causing damage to nature had been heard for many decades, it was in the 1970s that such voices became louder and more concerted, with numerous organizations being formed to preserve and protect the physical environment in which human pursuits, cultural as well as military and economic, took place. Part of this was a reaction against developmentalism: the wisdom of unlimited economic growth through industrialization and trade had come to be questioned when it was realized that these had taken place at the cost of polluting the air, water, and soil in all parts of the world; forests, rivers, and seabeds had been mercilessly subjected to exploitation, and rare animals, birds, and plants were becoming still more rare. Put this way, environmentalism was a devastating critique of modern civilization, a cultural movement that questioned some fundamental premises of recent history. It had thus the potentiality to develop into a global movement, coalescing people everywhere concerned with what appeared to be earth's diminishing resources. The Club of Rome, organized in 1973 with a commitment to warning against unrestricted economic growth, quickly established branches in many developed countries.

However, environmentalism in many ways straddled both the universalism that had sustained international cultural movements and the newer forces of multiculturalism, with their emphasis on diversity and pluralism. While the United Nations was, already in 1972, convening a conference on the human environment (which met in Stockholm), and while worldwide networks of environmentalists were fast being established to cooperate across national boundaries for the protection of the air, water, and endangered species, the decade of the 1970s also saw Third World countries arguing, more vociferously than ever, that the degradation of nature had been a result of the West's and Japan's relentless push for industrialization, and of their exploitation of the forests and rivers in other parts of the world. Third World spokesmen often argued that, although the Third World's own programs of economic modernization had added to the disaster, their transformation was a necessary response to the global penetration by advanced nations. A pattern of dependency relationships had been created in which Third World countries had become, willy-nilly, incorporated into a global system of production and consumption essentially as producers of primary goods, providers of cheap labor, and consumers of manufactured commodities imported from the industrialized nations.

The ideology of dependency combined with various other arguments to develop what some called Third Worldism, an outlook on international affairs in which the cultural identity of less-developed countries was seen to be defined in terms of the overwhelming influence of Western civilization. As Samir Amin argued in *Eurocentrism* (1989), not just the capitalist nations but also the Socialist countries of the West had influenced the Third World through their respective ideologies, through their shared stress on industrialization as a necessary means for nation building, and through the education of young men and women from Asia, Africa, and elsewhere in the universities and research institutes of the developed nations. Their outlooks had become Orientalist, to use the term made popular by Edward Said.[35] According to Said, since the Napoleonic era, people of the Orient had been accustomed to see themselves as the Other, the opposite of the West, which was taken as the norm. Oriental, and by extension Third World, self-definition had thus been determined by the West's identification of itself, and the Third World's destiny had been that of either remaining in this Other status, or of choosing to be more like the Occident. Developmentalism was a perfect example of this latter choice. But, as Cornelius Castoriadis has noted, development implied "a total transformation" of society—indeed, of man—so that it could lead to the obliteration of indigenous cultural traditions.[36]

For this reason, a growing number of Third World leaders, some even with a Western education, began actively opposing such a course for the future of their countries. Some used the concept of "cultural imperialism" to refer to the still dominant influence of Western civilization over the lives, behavior, and thought of people throughout the globe.[37] The concept gained adherents not just in the Third World but among the industrial countries.

The multiculturalist assault on cultural internationalism had to be squarely faced if this latter movement were to forge ahead in an age when cultural issues were steadily gaining in importance as determinants of international affairs. To persist in "past concepts of universality" was no longer tenable; this was the conclusion of a group of scholars from various parts of the world who met in 1972 to discuss "cultural relations for the future." There was a "clear historical trend," they asserted, "away from unilateral cultural relations, or the dissemination and imposition of a unified value system with implied universal and absolute validity, toward reciprocal cultural relations."[38] The principles of reciprocity and pluralism would, it was hoped, be able to accommodate the increasingly assertive Third World perspectives.

These voices, and many others like them, were evidence that in the decades after the 1970s, cultural internationalists everywhere sought to develop a world environment in which cultural diversity existed side by side with the awareness of shared values and concerns. If such an environment could be fostered, then cultural internationalism and multiculturalism would be made compatible; indeed, the two would reinforce each other. The United Nations University, to cite an example, undertook to establish networks of researchers who would study how different races, cultures, and social systems jointly could contribute to "the development of humanity." This, after all, had been the goal of interwar cultural internationalism, and in a sense the self-assertiveness of Third World countries could be said to make that vision a more realistic one, away from a predominantly Western-oriented definition.

In the meantime, changes in the United States and other advanced countries were potentially capable of accommodating cultural diversity without obliterating the awareness of shared values across national boundaries. The twin themes of cultural universalism and diversity were already becoming evident in U.S. society in the 1960s, which saw forces of diversity (ethnic minorities, women, advocates of so-called counterculture agendas) claiming a role for themselves in the name of universal values (justice, equality, democracy). As these forces multiplied, subdividing themselves into contending "cultures" and vying with each other for a share of power and influence, pluralism, traditionally the fundamental principle of democratic government, threatened to give way to separatism, even to disunity. By the 1990s observers were writing of "culture wars" in the United States as conflicting values seemed to characterize people's approaches to family life, education, and politics.[39]

Interestingly, the more U.S. society seemed to become divided ("disunited," as unhappy observers often pointed out), the greater grew its influence abroad. During the subsequent decades, while the United States domestically went through the trauma of the Vietnam debacle and public opinion shifted away from international commitments, geopolitically and economically, the process of global Americanization continued unabated. Indeed, in the 1970s and the 1980s, even as some began talking of the decline of the United States as a hegemonic power, the U.S. cultural influence was spreading with greater intensity than ever before—and not just to Europe and Japan but to the Socialist countries and to many Third World nations. Part of this was a product of the revolutionary changes in information and communications technology, most of them pioneered by U.S. engineers and entrepreneurs. The world was becoming more and more Americanized in that information emanating from the United States would be communicated instantly to other parts of the globe through satellite television and electronic mail.

Of course, there was resistance to this. In 1995, for instance, the government of India banned satellite dishes in that country, and other governments tried in various ways to limit the spread of worldwide information. UNESCO itself, under Third World initiatives, often sought to control access to, and transmission of, domestic information by Western journalists. But these efforts have never succeeded in preventing people everywhere from acquiring information about the wider world. Americanization, in the sense of shared information and, by implication, shared ideas and outlooks, is likely to continue, even as multiculturalism retains its strength.

Ultimately, however, it may be the cultural transformation of the United States and other democratic nations to which one has to look if the forces of multiculturalism are to be accommodated into a cultural internationalist agenda. It is premature to speculate about the nature of that transformation, but one may at least point to an undeniable demographic fact: the easing of geopolitical tensions since the 1970s has generated waves of cross-national, cross-continental migrants, as political refugees, religious minorities, and economically marginalized groups have breached national boundaries, contributing to the diversification of national populations.

Movements of people from less-advanced to more-developed economies have been massive, creating ethnic enclaves and often giving rise to interethnic tensions. Because the presence of a large number of foreigners is a politically sensitive issue, attention has tended to focus on the negative aspects of population migrations. But this phenomenon is also significant in the context of cultural internationalism, because the migrants inevitably bring with them their habits of thought and ways of life, thereby enriching the cultural life of the host countries. It is undoubtedly true, as Pierre Bourdieu has noted, that cultural products do not automatically reach all segments of the population; there often exists a hierarchy of cultural taste and judgment corresponding to a hierarchy of social and political status.[40] The fact remains that cultural expressions and institutions in the United States, Europe, and Japan have become steadily more diverse, making these societies that much more multicultural. (One may see this most graphically in food. Dietary habits in the West today are far more varied than only a decade or two ago, thanks to the influx of immigrants with different culinary traditions. The World Association of Cooks' Societies, organized in 1928, with a mostly European membership, to bring an international group of chefs together, today boasts a membership of one and a half million, and functions in fifty-two countries.) To the extent, therefore, that multiculturalism and cultural internationalism are mediated through the influx of migrants, one may talk of global and domestic multiculturalism as a positive force for internationalism.

Another notable phenomenon of the recent decades, the growth of ethnic and religious groups as well as nongovernmental organizations all over the world, can be understood in the same context. These bodies may be subsumed under the heading of cultural forces, because they challenge the authority of politically defined states preoccupied with security considerations and at the same time aim at goals other than increases in national wealth. Rather, they are concerned with preserving ethnic and religious heritages and with cooperating across national boundaries for humanitarian and other ends. The self-assertiveness by ethnic and religious minorities, not just in Third World countries but also in the West, strengthens multiculturalism, nationally and internationally. Some of them have been separatist and exclusionary, even prone to violence—something that is certainly not compatible with internationalism, or even with nationalism. It remains to be seen whether the rise in influence of these forces may prove to have the effect of promoting internationalism by undermining the authority of sovereign states, but without inviting anarchy.

One hopeful development in this connection has been the mushrooming of nongovernmental organizations (NGOs), numbering more than four hundred at the beginning of the 1990s. NGOs have taken over some functions earlier performed by states, many of which are cultural, broadly defined. For instance, a multinational group of physicians, Doctors without Borders, has been extremely active in combating contangious diseases in Africa, helping earthquake victims in Turkey, and treating victims of civil strife in various parts of the world. Environmentalists (Greenpeace and similar organizations) have been active in a campaign against the extermination of endangered species. A consortium of more than one hundred universities and businesses has been engaged in the development of a universally applicable "intelligence manufacturing system" that would standardize the process of designing, manufacturing, and distributing goods through the use of computers. All these activities transcend narrowly constructed national objectives and are truly global. I would not predict whether such efforts, rather than the potentially divisive forces of ethnic and religious communities, indicate the future direction of history; at least both phenomena suggest that recent years have steadily brought culture to a central position in national and international affairs.

The history of the world since World War II suggests that cultural diversity and cultural internationalism have related to each other in various ways. Each is likely to remain among the main forces of the world to come. Multiculturalism and Americanization are their contemporary manifestations.

Just as multiculturalism and Americanization need not be incompatible, cultural diversity and cultural internationalism may yet work out a pattern of association to define a stable world order. If one could incorporate the diversity of humanity into the agenda for internationalist programs—if one could develop a strategy for exchanges that were not unidirectional but multidirectional, maintaining open intellectual discourses with representatives of all cultural traditions in order to cope with environmental, demographic, and other urgent issues of the contemporary world, and strengthening nongovernmental multinational organizations in which various regions of the globe were represented—if such efforts could be made, then cultural internationalism would survive the turmoil of contemporary history and could point the way to a more interdependent, cooperative international community. The main obstacle to cultural internationalism, in such a perspective, would be not so much human diversity as national and parochial egoisms, not so much the opposition between the West and the Third World as exclusionary viewpoints in both.

Clearly, the global environment in which cultural internationalism operates has changed. Increasingly, cultural questions have joined geopolitical, trade, and other traditional issues in affecting the shape of the world. Security and trade matters will not go away, nor will nation-states with their individual quests for power and economic interests, no matter how outmoded the international system such conceptions presuppose may become. But international relations defined in power or economic terms are likely to be supplemented, if not superseded, by a culturally defined system of world order in which global networks of information, a shared concern over the natural environment, the awareness of the diverse ways in which men and women choose to live their lives, and cross-national efforts at combating poverty, disease, and illiteracy— and not just armaments or trade statistics—will come to constitute the "realities." The internationally conducted scientific research on global change—the study of climate conditions, ozone depletion, and the like—is estimated to cost trillions of dollars in the coming years.[41] If such a project, rather than the still persistent interethnic struggles, can be said to represent the way the world order is being reformulated, then it may be concluded that cultural internationalism will have a reinvigorated role to play in a system of international relations that increasingly is culturally defined.

Toward a Cultural Definition of International Relations

Two strikingly contrasting approaches have characterized recent studies of the history of international relations. On one hand, decision-making studies, the more traditional approach in which foreign policy and strategic decisions are scrutinized in great detail, have been enriched by the opening of archives in many parts of the world, especially the former Soviet Union and the People's Republic of China. A notable example in this regard is *Uncertain Partners* (1993), in which scholars from Russia, the United States, and China examine newly declassified material to trace in great detail how Joseph Stalin and Mao Tse-tung dealt with each other and with the United States during 1949–1950. In European international history, the decision-making approach on the basis of multi-archival research is exemplified by D.C. Watt's *How War Came* (1989), a detailed study of the coming of war in September 1939. The focus is sharply on decision makers, but there is much discussion of public opinion as well, insofar as it bears on official relations. Of course, since decisions must be based on realistic assessments of various nations' intentions and capabilities, works in this category usually examine such factors as military intelligence, industrial productivity, and economic mobilization. Alan S. Milward's *War, Economy, and Society* (1979) and Paul Kennedy's *The Rise and Fall of the Great Powers* (1985) are good examples. The former compares the different mobilizations of resources by the major powers in the 1930s; the latter traces how those powers have succeeded in achieving great-power status—and how some of them have lost it through a mismatch of ends and means. These studies offer careful analyses of comparative power positions against the background of the geopolitical realities at a given moment.

In contrast to these studies, centering on decision makers and geopolitical strategies, a second group of works is more "decentered" or "local" in the sense that they examine political, social, and intellectual settings within a country. These settings do not automatically translate themselves into specific policy decisions, but they do provide the context in which one country's relations with another are defined. Works in this category have been concerned not so much with governmental decisions, rational calculations of power, or economic mobilization as with ideas, emotions, moods, religious trends, gender relations, and the like that constitute the makeup of a society as it interacts with other societies. This approach has been influenced by social history, literary criticism, culture studies, and other disciplines that have produced penetrating case studies as well as large-scale interpretations. In contrast to the first approach, it is less oriented toward multiarchival work than toward delving deeply into the people and culture of one country, or even a subdivision of a country. Thus international relations tend to be seen as a reflection of domestic social conditions and ideologies—the "cultural productions" of the countries involved—not as an interaction of national actors that are essentially interchangeable. Paul Fussell's *Wartime*

(1989), for instance, focuses on the ideas and behavior of common soldiers in the United States and Britain during World War II and aims at examining what the war meant to them, not to their political leaders or to governmental spokesmen. Robert David Johnson's *Peace Progressives and American Foreign Relations* (1994), to cite another example, explores the ways in which certain U.S. senators defined their own conceptions of international affairs, in the framework of which they critiqued official policies.

The tension between the decision-making approach and the localized approach has been evident for some time. In a sense it is analogous to the controversy over the primacy of external versus internal politics that agitated historians of international relations a decade or two ago. Even the celebrated controversies over Fritz Fischer's *Germany's War Aims in the First World War* (1967; first published as *Griff nach der Weltmacht*, 1961) and over A. J. P. Taylor's *The Origins of the Second World War* (1961) can be put in the same framework; the former produced mountains of evidence concerning German ambitions and aspirations in the 1910s, while the latter sought to understand German foreign policy in the 1930s in the context of world power equations. The debate has been sharp because it concerns two contrasting ways of conceptualizing international affairs: as an interplay of world geopolitical forces, or as a product of local politics and imaginations.

Put this way, the challenge has been somehow to try to bring the two perspectives together; to develop a scheme in which local forces integrate themselves into a global situation. This is what theorists of international relations have begun to try by applying postmodernist critique to world politics.[1] As yet, few convincing arguments or methodologies have been advanced.

Historians of international relations, in the meantime, have produced a few suggestive monographs. David Kaiser's *Politics and War* (1990), for instance, is an ambitious attempt at linking political developments within a number of European states to a regional "climate of opinion," and the latter in turn to world affairs, from the sixteenth century to the twentieth. Narrower in focus in time and space, Frank Ninkovich's *Modernity and Power* (1994) analyzes the domino theory, which underlay U.S. foreign policy in the twentieth century, as a series of responses to the global economic and technological changes that redefined world power realities at the beginning of the century.

A somewhat different framework emerges in a book like Ron Robin's *Enclaves of America* (1992), a study of U.S. embassies and cemeteries overseas as expressions of ideas about the nation's position in the world. In *Enclaves*, Robin is trying to get out of the usual geopolitical frameworks (the cold war and the Vietnam War, for example) and instead to trace the history of the making of monuments as a more enduring aspect of U.S. relations with other countries.

What a book like Robin's suggests is that domestic and global developments may be connected, not necessarily in terms of a geopolitically defined international system but of a culturally conceptualized world order. We may in fact need a new conceptualization of international relations if we are to inquire seriously into the roles played by ideas, aspirations, and emotions in the world. They "invent" a world just as geopolitical factors do, but these worlds are not identical. To study the one, we should not apply the conceptualizations and methodologies adopted for the other. In other words, cross-national cultural forces and developments, linking the societies and peoples of different countries, can never be fully understood in a framework of geopolitics, economic mobilization, security, strategy, and the like. One needs an alternative definition of international relations, a definition of world affairs not as an arena of interstate power rivalries but as a field for interdependent forces and movements, not as a structure of power relations but as a social context for interchanges among individuals and groups across national boundaries. If such a cultural formulation were adopted, it would become easier to link international to domestic affairs. The latter, too, in that context, would take on fresh significance. It would be not so much in terms of their impact on national politics or decision making as in terms of their producing forces that would create cultural borderlands and contribute to global change that domestic forces would be linked to the larger world.

Before going farther with the cultural definition of international relations, we may note the economic definition that, along with the geopolitical, has played an important role in the historiographical literature. The conceptual framework of a world economic system, in which each nation, its people, products, and capital play various roles individually and in conjunction with other countries, provides an important perspective in which national and international affairs may be closely linked. However, to the extent that a nation's economic resources and interests are seen as part of its power and as objects of its foreign policy, the study of international relations in such a framework differs little from the geopolitical approach.

At the same time, there is a cultural aspect to such phenomena. As Oscar Handlin has noted, U.S. business entrepreneurs at the turn of the twentieth century developed a notion of "one world" as they literally linked the nation to all parts of the globe through their commercial and investment activities.[2] Economic internationalism in theory and practice was thus as much a cultural formulation as a business proposition. Michael Hogan, to take another example, has demonstrated in *The Making of the Marshall Plan* (1990) that "corporatist" arrangements in the United States and Western Europe—a pattern of close cooperation between state and society—made possible a definition of trans-Atlantic relations in which an open system of economic transactions would promote the overall well-being of the region and the world. Of course, to the extent that the Marshall Plan fitted into the cold war strategy of the United States, it can be examined in the geopolitical framework, but in order to connect it to domestic developments, the corporatist approach is useful, and what it offers is essentially a cultural definition of national and international affairs.

What I have proposed in this book is to explore further possibilities for a cultural definition of international relations as a way to link national developments to world developments. Because a nation is a cultural construction, it can be conceptually linked to the world only if the latter, too, is conceptualized in cultural terms.

"Alter ideas and you alter the world," H. G. Wells asserted in 1930. "Children can be taught that the conquest of knowledge, the establishment of world order, the attainment of human health and happiness, are finer ends than pulling down and tearing up one flag in order to hoist another."[3] Wells's ideas did not "alter the world," but that does not mean that his visions, combined with those of countless others all over the world, were not creating an alternative world, a world that was removed from the "realities" but was nevertheless more "realistic" to them. Seven years later (1937), a Labour member of Parliament, speaking about the United Kingdom, lamented, "This country will be conquered, not by the sword, but by the invasion of American finances and American thought."[4] He was paying greater attention to a world becoming unified under U.S. cultural influence than to one in which totalitarian states were threatening the peace. To him, and to Wells, a culturally defined international community was as "real" as the world dominated by geopolitical considerations.

A cultural definition of international relations seems particularly pertinent today. To be sure, much is made of the alleged "chaos" that is said to have ensued in the aftermath of the cold war. But it is not really a chaos at all if one views international affairs as a cultural phenomenon. It simply means that, now that military power, strategy, mobilization for war, and alliance diplomacy have lost their once dominant roles in defining international relations, other forces, social and cultural, are coming to the fore. These forces have always existed, however, and shaped the contemporary world. They have not been noticed or given due scholarly attention because of the preoccupation with the geopolitical realities of international affairs. But by adopting the cultural perspective, it would become possible to write a different sort of international history.

This book is an attempt at such reexamination of the past. Its overall framework has been a conceptualization of international relations as a cultural construction. I have tried to examine cultural interactions, broadly put, among nations with a view to getting at the assumptions, latent if not always clearly articulated, underlying such interactions. What the preceding chapters reveal, I think, is a long history of the quest for alternative meanings, for fresh perspectives on international relations.

From the seventeenth century onward, jurists intent on codifying laws governing the conduct of nations toward one another as well as philosophers and economists interested in promoting world trade had a conception of an interdependent community of nations that were, at least in theory, in harmony and mutually compatible. In the late nineteenth century and the early twentieth century, varieties of internationalism were developed as self-conscious movements for overcoming inter-state rivalries that were producing more and more efficient military forces and kept nations in a state of constant preparedness for war. Of various internationalist proposals, particularly notable were the beginnings of cultural internationalism, exemplified by such moves as the exchange of information, coordination of weights and measures, and the organization of international associations of scientists and doctors.

A cultural definition of international relations developed with full force in the wake of World War I, when educators, intellectuals, artists, musicians, and many others cooperated across national boundaries to promote mutual understanding. They envisioned a world in which the exchange of students and scholars, collaborative intellectual enterprises, artistic exhibits, symposia on current affairs, and similar undertakings would take the place of arms races and military alliances as determinants of international affairs. The development of mass-communications technology—notably, the telephone, the radio, and the cinema—seemed to justify such optimism. The optimism, of course, proved premature, but even in the 1930s, when armament, war, and excessive nationalism returned with an unprecedented ferocity, the cultural underpinnings of international relations were never lost sight of, in the totalitarian states as elsewhere. In the democracies, although geopolitical realism made a comeback, it was not entirely successful in stifling ongoing efforts to keep alive the flames of cultural internationalism.

The flames have survived World War II and the cold war and today are claiming much attention as a possible solution to the chaos in the world. Cultural internationalism has, in the past fifty years, undergone transformation. Compared with its prewar antecedent, it is more comprehensive, reflecting the self-conscious diversity of the world in which non-Europeans have been increasingly active in cultural affairs. Cultural internationalists are now concerned with such matters as human rights, environmental protection, and the preservation of endangered species, issues that were not taken up earlier. By thus broadening its scope, cultural internationalism may again be serving to redefine international relations.

The abortive attempt of the 1920s was followed by a violent reaction. To avoid a repetition of that history, cultural internationalists in all countries will need to struggle against cultural chauvinists as well as geopolitical nationalists; that is, both against parochial tendencies that deny possibilities for cross-cultural communication and against policy formulations that give primacy to military considerations. This is an extremely difficult task, but the history of cultural internationalism shows heroic efforts by pioneers who stood on cultural ground and worked hard to broaden cultural borderlands. The principles of "universality, permanence, and independence" that some of them asserted in 1937 are still valid today. The universality of shared values and concerns, the permanence of the commitment to promoting cross-cultural communication and cooperation unhindered by changing intellectual fashions, and independence from the dictates of state policies or geopolitical interests—if these principles could be followed in as many nations as possible, then there might eventually emerge an international order in which culture was restored to its central place.[5]

Introduction

1. See my essay, "Culture and International History," in Michael Hogan, ed., *Explaining the History of American Foreign Relations* (New York, 1991), 215.

2. F. M. Hinsley, *Power and the Pursuit of Peace: Theory and Practice in the History of Relations between States* (Cambridge, 1963), 57.

3. Frank Ninkovich, *Modernity and Power: A History of the Domino Theory in the Twentieth Century* (Chicago, 1994), 8–10.

4. Robert Park, *Race and Culture* (Boston, 1940), 151.

5. Manley O. Hudson, *Current International Cooperation* (Calcutta, 1927), 11.

6. Warren Susman, *Culture as History: The Transformation of American Society in the Twentieth Century* (New York, 1984).

7. Quoted in Krishan Kumar, *Utopia and Anti-Utopia in Modern Times* (Oxford, 1987), 288.

8. Reinhold Wagnleitner, *Coca-Colonization and the Cold War: The Cultural Mission of the United States in Austria after the Second World War* (Chapel Hill, N.C., 1995).

9. Jacob van Staaveren, *An American in Japan: A Civilian View of the Occupation* (Seattle, 1994), 22.

10. Quoted in James Der Derian, *On Diplomacy: A Genealogy of Western Estrangement* (Oxford, 1987), 116.

O N E :   The Internationalist Imagination

1. Leon Trotsky, *The Balkan Wars* (New York, 1980), 64, 79–80; Leon Trotsky, *Sochineniia* (Moscow, 1925), 4:97–98, 106; Leon Trotsky, *My Life* (New York, 1930), 226.

2. Leon Trotsky, *Gody velikogo pereloma* (Moscow, 1919), 162–63.

3. Benedict Anderson, *Imagined Communities: Reflections on the Origin and Spread of Nationalism* (New York, 1991); Declan Kiberd, *Inventing Ireland* (Cambridge, Mass., 1996).

4. Henry Thomas Buckle, *History of Civilization in England* (New York, 1906), 1:137. For a discussion of the ancient Roman emphasis on military victory as the legitimating principle for rulership, see Michael McCormick, *Eternal Victory: Triumphal Rulership in Late Antiquity, Byzantium, and the Early Medieval West* (Cambridge, 1986).

5. Trotsky, *Balkan Wars*, 67.

6. Cited in Bernard Semmel, *Liberalism and Naval Strategy: Ideology, Interest, and Sea Power during the Pax Britannica* (Boston, 1986), 68.

7. For an excellent discussion of the ideas of war and peace developed by Kant and the Manchester liberals, see W. B. Gallie, *Philosophers of Peace and War: Kant, Clausewitz, Marx, Engeles, and Tolstoy* (Cambridge, 1978). See also E. H. Carr, *Twenty Years' Crisis, 1919–1939: An Introduction to the Study of International Relations* (London, 1939), 25.

8. Lord Acton, *The History of Freedom and Other Essays* (London, 1904), 270–300.

9. Michael Howard, *The Causes of Wars and Other Essays* (London, 1983), 27–28. There is an enormous volume of literature on nineteenth-century nationalism. Among the most perceptive recent studies are E. J. Hobsbawm, *Nations and Nationalism since 1870: Programme, Myth, Reality* (Cambridge, 1990) and David Kaiser, *Politics and War: European Conflict from Philip II to Hitler* (Cambridge, Mass., 1990). See especially Kaiser, 271–325.

10. P. E. Corbett, *Law and Society in the Relations of States* (New York, 1951), 36; F. M. Hinsley, *Power and the Pursuit of Peace: Theory and Practice in the History of Relations between States* (Cambridge, 1963), 166. See also Terry Nardin and David R. Mapel, eds., *Traditions of International Ethics* (Cambridge, 1992), 34–35.

11. Henry Wheaton, *Elements of International Law*, 4th ed. (Lon-

don, 1904), 24. On the idea of European civilization at the end of the nineteenth century, see J. M. Blaut, *The Colonizer's Model of the World: Geographical Diffusionism and Eurocentric History* (New York, 1993). Among the most authoritative studies of international law in the nineteenth century and its relationship to the concept of civilization are Gerrit W. Gong, *The Standard of 'Civilization' in International Society* (Oxford, 1984) and Hedley Bull and Adam Watson, eds., *The Expansion of International Society* (Oxford, 1984). See particularly Hedley Bull's essays in this latter volume.

12. Urbain Gohier, *La Révolution, vient-elle?* (Paris, 1908) 160–194.

13. Urbain Gohier, *Le Peuple des XXe siècle aux Etats Unis* (Paris, 1903), 20–23, 156–59.

14. Gustave Hervé, *L'Internationalisme* (Paris, 1910), 167–78. Hervé's stress on international migration of capital and labor was pushed to its logical extremes by H. G. Wells on the eve of World War I. In one of his numerous writings prophesying the future world, Wells wrote, "Every country finds a growing section of its home-born people either living largely abroad, drawing the bulk of their income from the exterior, and having their essential interests wholly or partially across the frontier." Such being the case, there was likely to emerge "a new kind of people, a floating population going about the world, uprooted, delocalised, and even, it may be, denationalised, with wide interests and wide views, developing, no doubt, customs and habits of its own, a morality of its own, a philosophy of its own." These ideas were to form the basis of Wells's cosmopolitanism after World War I. See H. G. Wells, *An Englishman Looks at the World* (London, 1914), 19, 20.

15. Cited in Drew McCoy, *The Elusive Republic: Political Economy in Jeffersonian America* (Chapel Hill, N.C., 1980), 87.

16. Herbert Spencer, *Principles of Sociology* (1876; New York, 1926), 607–28.

17. H. L. S. Lyons, *Internationalism in Europe, 1815–1914* (Leiden, Netherlands, 1963), 14, 125–26.

18. Leonard Woolf, *International Government* (London, 1916), 174–75; Friedrich Naumann, *Mitteleuropa,* English translation (New York, 1917), 184. See also Harold James, *A German Identity, 1770–1990,* (New York, 1989), 106. On women's organizations, see Leila J. Rupp, "Constructing Internationalism," in *American Historical Review* 99:1571–1600 (Dec. 1994).

19. Lyons, *Internationalism*, 15–16. On the influence of Oriental art and architecture at world's fairs, see John M. MacKenzie, *Orientalism: History, Theory, and the Arts* (Manchester, 1995).

20. *Annales internationales d'histoire* (Paris, 1899), xi–xx; FO371/7053/W10357, Foreign Office archives, Public Record Office, London.

21. Amy Kaplan and Donald E. Pease, eds., *Cultures of United States Imperialism* (Durham, N.C., 1993), 145–46.

22. *La vie internationale* 1, no. 1 (1912): 5, 7, 33, 34.

23. James Joll, *The Origins of the First World War* (London, 1992), 206–7; Gallie, *Philosophers*, 69–70.

24. Zeev Sternhell, *The Birth of Fascist Ideology: From Cultural Rebellion to Political Revolution* (Princeton, 1994), 197.

25. Sondra Herman, *Eleven against War: Studies in American Internationalist Thought, 1890–1921* (Stanford, Calif., 1969), 126–37.

26. Joll, *Origins*, 213.

27. Thomas Willig Balch, *Eméric Crucé* (Philadelphia, 1900), 27–28, 33–34.

28. *Nihon rekishi* (Japanese history) 16 (Tokyo, 1976): 26. See also James Turner Johnson, *The Quest for Peace: Three Moral Traditions in Western Cultural History* (Princeton, 1987), 268–69.

29. *International Congress of Arts and Science, vol. 3* (Boston, 1906): 663.

30. Rupp, *AHR*, Dec. 1994, 1576.

31. Suzuki Akira, *1936-nen Berlin shikyūden* (1936, an urgent telegram from Berlin) (Tokyo, 1994), 54.

32. Miwa Kimitada, *Nihon 1945-nen no shiten* (Japan, a 1945 perspective) (Tokyo, 1986), v.

33. Cited in Akira Iriye, *Nihon no gaikō* (Japanese diplomacy) (Tokyo, 1965), 7.

34. Zara Steiner, *Britain and the Origins of the World War* (London, 1977), 16.

35. François Coppé, *Dans l'espirt de la revanche* (Paris, 1915), 194–95.

36. *Congress of Arts and Science*, vol. 2 (Boston, 1906): 107–8. On Chamberlain, the best recent study is Ōta Yūzō's *B. H. Chamberlain* (Tokyo, 1990); on Fenollosa, see Lawrence Chisolm, *Fenollosa: The Far East and American Culture* (New Haven, Conn., 1963). On the 1911 congress, see "First Universal Races Congress" (London, 1911), a pamphlet prepared for the occasion.

37. George Oshiro, *Nitobe Inazō* (Tokyo, 1993), 46. Nitobe's lecture tour was also sponsored by the fledgling Japan Society, established in New York in 1907 for "the cultivation of friendly relations" between the two countries.

38. Inazo Nitobe, *The Japanese Nation* (New York, 1912), 2–3.

39. *Asakawa Kan'ichi shokanshū* (Letters of Asakawa Kan'ichi) (Tokyo, 1990), 11, 195–96.

40. Jung-pang Lo, *K'ang Yu-wei* (Tucson, Ariz., 1967), 348.

41. Hirakawa Sukehiro and Tsuruta Kin'ya, eds., *Uchinaru kabe* (Walls within) (Tokyo, 1990), 61; Jawaharlal Nehru, *Toward Freedom* (Boston, 1967), 29–30.

42. Stuart Anderson, *Race and Rapprochement: Anglo-Saxonism and Anglo-American Relations, 1895–1904* (Rutherford, N.J., 1981); Steiner, *Britain*, 17.

43. Hinsley, *Power and Principle*, 50.

T W O : The Origins of Cultural Internationalism

1. Gustave Hervé, *La patrie en danger* (Paris, 1915), 43–44, 49.

2. Urbain Gohier, *La race a parlé* (Paris, 1916), 3, 41, 64–66.

3. Richard Dehmel, *Zwischen Volk und Menschheit* (Berlin, 1919).

4. Sigmund Graff, *Unvergessliche Krieg* (Leipzig, [1936]), 125.

5. Bernard Shaw, *Complete Plays with Prefaces* (New York, 1963), 1:451.

6. Rudolf Hoffmann, *Der Deutsche Soldat: Briefe aus dem Weltkrieg* (Munich, 1937), 101, 109, 292.

7. Ernst Johannsen, *Vier von der Infantrie* (Hamburg, 1920), 49.

8. Jean François Sirinelli, *Intellectuels et passions françaises: Manifestes et petitions au XXe siècle* (Paris, 1990), 41–42.

9. League of Nations, "Moral Disarmament," February 24, 1932, ED25/25, Board of Education Archives, Public Record Office, London.

10. Thomas J. Knock, *To End All Wars: Woodrow Wilson and the Quest for a New World Order* (New York, 1992).

11. M. K. Follett, *The New State: Group Organization the Solution of Popular Government* (London, 1918); William Y. Elliott, *The Pragmatic Revolt in Politics: Syndicalism, Fascism, and the Constitutional State* (New York, 1928).

12. Follett, *The New State*, 3, 348.

13. *Atlantic* 141 (February 1928), 157; Henry Ford, *My Philosophy*

of Industry (London, 1929): Reinhold Niebuhr, "Perils of American Power," *Atlantic* 149 (January 1932): 90–95.

14. Follett, *The New State,* 345–46.

15. Heath memo, May 25, 1929, ED25/25.

16. Cited in Akira Iriye, *Across the Pacific: An Inner History of American-East Asian Relations* (New York, 1967), 145.

17. Maurice Leenhardt, *Le prestige du Blanc menacé* (Paris, 1929), 24.

18. FO371/8335/W9237, September 29, 1922; FO371/5486/W3259, December 10, 1920.

19. FO371/8308/W10463, August 5, 1922; FO371/8308/W2564, March 16, 1922.

20. British national committee meeting, November 6, 1931, ED25/25.

21. *Kokusai bunka* (International culture), no. 1 (November 1938): 4.

22. The papers of James Shotwell (Columbia University) are the best source for the activities of the U.S. national committee on intellectual cooperation.

23. Amy Kaplan and Donald E. Pease, eds., *Cultures of United States Imperialism* (Durham, N.C., 1993), 16.

24. British national committee meeting, February 25, 1931, ED25/25.

25. Robert F. Byrnes, *Awakening American Education to the World: The Role of Archibald Cary Coolidge, 1866–1928* (Notre Dame, Ind., 1982), 184.

26. Mortimer Graves, "A Sketch of the Development of the American Council of Learned Societies," *ACLS Newsletter,* 1955.

27. William Y. Elliott, *The New British Empire* (New York, 1932), 12.

28. Cited in Dorothy Ross, *The Origins of American Social Science* (Cambridge, 1991), 438.

29. The story is well recounted in Kristin Thompson, *Exporting Entertainment: America in the World Film Market, 1907–34* (London, 1985); and David Strauss, *Menace in the West: The Rise of French Anti-Americanism in Modern Times* (Westport, 1978). See also John T. Trumpbour, "'Death to Hollywood'" (Ph.D. diss., Harvard University, 1996).

30. Heath memo, Dec. 9, 1929, ED25/25.

31. Fred Fejes, *Imperialism, Media, and the Good Neighbor: New Deal Foreign Policy and United States Short Wave Broadcasting to Latin America* (Norwood, N.J., 1980), 19–20.

32. FO371/18546/W429 contains many documents on a possible international "agreement for use of broadcasting in the cause of peace."

33. British national committee meeting, December 9, 1929, ED25/25; British national committee meeting, October 3, 1930, ibid.; See Heng Teow, "Japan's Cultural Policy toward China, 1918–1931" (Ph.D. diss., Harvard University, 1993).

34. Jean François Sirinelli, *Génération intellectuelle: Khâgneux et normaliens dans l'entre-deux-guerres* (Paris, 1988), 541–42.

35. Foreign Office, ed., *Gaimushō no hyakunen* (One hundred years of the Foreign Office) (Tokyo, 1969), 1:1039–45.

36. See See Heng Teow's essay in Robert David Johnson, ed., *On Cultural Ground: Essays in International History* (Chicago, 1994), 147–71.

37. Fujii Shōzō, *Tōkyō gaigo Shina-bu* (The Tokyo Language School's Chinese department) (Tokyo, 1992), 67–69.

38. John E. Farquharson and Stephen C. Holt, *Europe from Below: An Assessment of Franco-German Popular Contacts* (London, 1975), 64.

39. International Committee on Intellectual Cooperation report, 1927, ED25/25.

40. British national committee meeting, April 15, 1932, ibid.

41. FO371/16441/W10445, August 20, 1932.

42. FO371/5486/W3328, December 9, 1920.

43. FO370/531/L519, July 30–August 6, 1938.

44. FO371/7053/W10357 September 14, 1921.

45. British national committee meeting, November 6, 1926, ED25/25.

46. Robert S. Schwantes, *Japanese and Americans: A Century of Cultural Relations* (New York, 1955), 9.

47. *Bulletin of the American Women's Club of Paris*, October 1928.

48. Benjamin March, *China and Japan in American Museums* (New York, 1929), 27.

49. *World Unity*, April 1930: 28–29.

50. On the efforts to solve the immigration question after 1924, see Izumi Hirobe, "American Attitudes toward the Immigration Question, 1924–1931," *Journal of American-East Asian Relations* 2 (fall 1993): 275–301.

51. Robert and Helen Lynd, *Middletown: A Study in Contemporary Culture* (New York, 1929), 261–65.

52. Horace M. Kallen, *Culture and Democracy in the United States* (New York, [1924]), 64.

53. Robert Park, *Race and Culture* (Boston, 1940), 144, 148–9.

54. Paul Johnson, *Modern Times: The World from the Twenties to the Eighties* (New York, 1983).

55. See Frederick Starr, *Red and Hot: The Fate of Jazz in the Soviet Union, 1917–1980* (New York, 1983).

56. Joshua Fogel, *Nakae Ushikichi in China: The Mourning of Spirit* (Cambridge, Mass., 1989).

57. Jawaharlal Nehru, *Toward Freedom* (Boston, 1967), 230–31.

58. Josef Stalin, *Fundamentals of Leninism* (New York, 1939), 122–24. An extremely interesting phenomenon in post-Revolutionary Russia was the development of Eurasianism, the idea that the Soviet Union comprised both Europeans and Asians within its borders; both were authentic members of the community as they shared the same history. Roman Szporluk notes a similarity betwen the Eurasianism of the late 1920s and the ideas of Wells. See Roman Szporluk, "The Eurasia House: Problems of Identity in Russia and Eastern Europe," *Cross Currents* 9: 13 (1990).

59. Frank Ninkovich, *Modernity and Power: A History of the Domino Theory in the Twentieth Century* (Chicago, 1994), 69.

60. *Congressional Record,* 67th Congress, 1st session (April 20, 1921), 61, pt 1: 515.

61. Manley O. Hudson, *Current International Cooperation* (Calcutta, 1927), 11.

62. H. G. Wells, *The Way to World Peace* (London, 1930), 13. For an excellent discussion of the internationalism of J. A. Hobson who shared some of Wells' optimism at this time, see David Long, "J. A. Hobson and Idealism in International Relations," *Review of International Studies,* 17: 285–304 (1991).

THREE: The Separation of Culture from Internationalism

1. William Shirer, *The Nightmare Years* (New York, 1985).

2. H. G. Wells, *The Way to World Peace* (London, 1930), 31; Frank Ninkovich, *Modernity and Power: A History of the Domino Theory in the Twentieth Century* (Chicago, 1994), 120.

3. FO371/16440/W6908, June 7, 1932, Public Record Office.

4. Michael Burleigh and Wolfgang Wippermann, *The Racial State: Germany 1933–1945* (Cambridge, 1991).

5. Ibid., 206. Recall the famous line attributed to Hermann Goering: "Whenever I hear the word culture, I reach for my pistol." The line's original version is in Hanns Johst, *Schlageter* (Munich, 1934), act 1, scene 1.

6. On Carl von Ossietzky, see *New York Times,* January 13, 1996: 2. On Wilhelm Furtwängler, see his *Notebooks, 1924–1950* (London, 1989), 155.

7. Edgar Maass, *Verdun* (Berlin, 1936), 252.

8. Joachim von der Goltz, *Der Baum von Cléry* (Munich, 1934), 144, 185, 195.

9. Konrad Heiden, *Hitler: A Biography* (Zurich, 1936), 87.

10. Robert Tucker, *Stalin in Power: The Revolution from Above, 1928–1941* (New York, 1990), 353, 479–584.

11. Reinhold Niebuhr, *Reflections on the End of an Era* (New York, 1934), 16–18, 28–29.

12. Janet Flanner, *Paris Was Yesterday: 1925–1939* (New York, 1972), 218–19.

13. William Y. Elliott, *The New British Empire* (New York, 1932), 15.

14. William A. Orton, *America in Search of Culture* (Boston, 1933), 256.

15. Warren Susman, *Culture as History: The Transformation of American Society in the Twentieth Century* (New York, 1984); Richard Pells, *Radical Visions and American Dreams: Culture and Social Thought in the Depression Years* (Middletown, Conn., 1973). See also Robert David Johnson, *Peace Progressives and American Foreign Relations* (Cambridge, Mass., 1994).

16. British national commitee meeting, October 6, 1931, ED25/25.

17. FO371/18545/W8218, July 16–21, 1934.

18. John E. Farquharson and Stephen C. Holt, *Europe from Below: An Assessment of Franco-German Popular Contacts* (London, 1975), 64.

19. FO371/18545/W8218, July 16–21, 1934.

20. Li Chang, "I-chiu-san-ling nien-tai Chung-kuo yü Kuo-lien ti chi-shu ho-tsuo" (China's technical cooperation with the League of Nations during the 1930s), *Bulletin of the Institute of Modern History* 15, pt. 2 (Dec. 1986):281–314.

21. Maruyama Kumao, *1930-nendai no Paris to watakushi* (Paris and I in the 1930s) (Tokyo, 1986). The best record of U.S.-Japan student conferences is *Kaisen zen'ya no discussion* (Discussions on the eve of the war) (Tokyo, 1984).

22. William Peterson, *Passport to Friendship: The Story of the Experiment in International Living* (Philadelphia, 1957), 78. It is interesting to note that in 1992 the Experiment in International Living, then administering 260 different programs in sixty-seven countries, changed its name to World Learning, Inc.

23. FO370/553/L5958, August 16, 1938.

24. FO395/510/P1263, April 23, 1934.

25. FO924/294/LC94, November 29, 1945.

26. Eugen Weber, *The Hollow Years: France in the 1930s* (New York, 1994), 8.

27. "Moral Disarmament," February 24, 1932, ED25/25.

28. FO371/18545/W8218, 1934.

29. FO371/21250/16679, August 9, 1937.

30. Ibid.

31. Minutes of July 17, 1939 meeting, Shotwell Papers.

32. Bonnet to Kenyon, September 4, 1939, ED25/8.

33. Malcolm Cowley, *The Dream of the Golden Mountains: Remembering the 1930s* (New York, 1964), 218.

34. "Humanities—Program and Policy" (Agenda for Special Trustees' Meeting, April 11, 1935), R.G.3, Rockefeller Foundation Archives.

35. John T. McGreevy, *Parish Boundaries: The Catholic Encounter with Race in the Twentieth-Century Urban North* (Chicago, 1996), 44.

36. Irwin Gellman, *Good Neighbor Diplomacy: United States Policies in Latin America, 1933–1945* (Baltimore, 1979), 64–65.

37. Cherrington's essay in *Think* 6, no. 4 (April 1940).

38. Cherrington to Ware, April 22, 1941, Shotwell Papers.

39. Robert David Johnson, ed., *On Cultural Ground: Essays in International History* (Chicago, 1994), 173–96.

40. Rothschild to Thomson, August 10, 1940, Papers of Ben M. Cherrington, University of Denver; Cherrington to Thomson, April 16, 1941, ibid.

41. Frank Ninkovich, *The Diplomacy of Ideas: U.S. Foreign Policy and Cultural Relations, 1938–1950* (New York, 1981).

42. See Donald Fleming and Bernard Bailyn, eds., *Intellectual Migration: Europe and America, 1930–1960* (Cambridge, Mass. 1969).

43. FO370/531/L519, July 30–August 6, 1938.

44. FO370/531/L519/416/403, March 18, 1938.

45. Akira Iriye, *China and Japan in the Global Context* (Cam-

bridge, Mass., 1992), 84; Matsumoto Tsuyoshi, *Ryakudatsushita bunka* (Plundered cultures) (Tokyo, 1993), 48–50.

46. Iriye, *China and Japan,* 77–78.

47. See Akira Iriye, "Hsinminhui," in Akira Iriye, ed., *The Chinese and the Japanese: Essays in Political and Cultural Interactions* (Princeton, 1980), 254–74.

48. Fujisawa Chikao, *Zentaishugi to kōdō* (Totalitarianism and the imperial way) (Tokyo, 1939), 192–93.

49. IMT 135, LPS Doc. 956, Papers of International Military Tribunal for the Far East.

50. *Kokusai bunka,* no. 2 (January 1939): 4–6.

51. Ibid., no. 4 (May 1939): 9–12.

52. See Mark Peattie, *Ishiwara Kanji and Japan's Confrontation with the West* (Princeton, 1975), 67–74.

53. Ministry of Education, *Kokutai no hongi* (The essence of the nation) (Tokyo, 1937).

54. Uda Hisashi, *Tai-Shi bunka kōsaku sōan* (A draft cultural policy toward China) (Tokyo, 1939), 27–35.

55. See Iriye, *China and Japan,* 80–82, for examples of Japanese intellectuals' responses to the Chinese war.

56. Akira Iriye, *Nijusseiki no sensō to heiwa* (War and peace in the twentieth century) (Tokyo, 1986), 120–23.

57. Aurel Kolnai, *The War against the West* (London, 1938) contains numerous examples of German writing in the 1930s. For Carl Schmitt's theory of the state, see his "Reich-Staat-Bund," in *Positionen und Begriffe* (Hamburg, 1940).

58. For information concerning Nazi Germany's views of Japan and its culture, I am indebted to Harumi Furuya, "Ideology and Realpolitik" (unpublished bachelor's thesis, Harvard University, 1996).

59. *Harper's* 169 (August 1934): 268; Harper's 169 (September 1934): 426.

60. Pells, *Radical Visions,* 106–108.

61. Cowley, *Dream,* ix.

62. Pells, *Radical Visions,* 314–18.

63. Reinhold Niebuhr, *Christianity and Power Politics* (New York, 1940), 16–17.

64. Grover Smith, ed., *Letters of Aldous Huxley* (London, 1969), 411.

65. Robert Aron, *La fin de l'après-querre* (Paris, 1938), 79.

66. Ministry of Education, *Kokutai no hongi.*
67. Norman Angell, *For What Do We Fight?* (London, 1939), 1, 89.

F O U R :   The Cultural Foundations of the New Globalism

1. *New Republic* 105 (July 7, 1941): 17–18.
2. Haruyama Yukio, *Manshū no bunka* (The culture of Manchuria) (Tokyo, 1943), 6, 47, 303.
3. Saitō Shōji, *Gaisetsu Daitōaken* (A survey of the great East Asian region) (Tokyo, 1941), 11, 20, 28.
4. *Tribune* (Manila), July 20, 1944.
5. Grant Goodman, *Japanese Cultural Policies in Southeast Asia during World War Two* (New York, 1991).
6. Akira Iriye, *Power and Culture: The Japanese-American War, 1941–1945* (Cambridge, Mass., 1981), 118–20.
7. David Mitrany, *A Working Peace System* (London, 1946), 17.
8. E. H. Carr, *Conditions of Peace* (New York, 1944), xxiii–xxiv.
9. *New Republic* 105 (August 25, 1941), 238.
10. United Nations Charter, art. 62.
11. Zimmern's memo, no date, FO 924/294/LC106. For Zimmern's internationalism, see Paul Rich, "Alfred Zimmern's Cautious Idealism," in David Long and Peter Wilson, eds., *Thinkers of the Twenty Years' Crisis: Inter-War Idealism Reassessed* (Oxford, 1995). This volume contains excellent essays on some of the British internationalists I discuss: E. H. Carr, Norman Angell, Leonard Woolf.
12. Ware to Bonnet, September 24, 1941, Shotwell Papers.
13. FO 924/230/LC2287, May 26, 1945.
14. The only systematic study of the wartime meetings of allied education ministers is Denis Mylonas, *La genèse de l'UNESCO: La conférence des ministres alliés de l'éducation, 1942–1945* (Brussels, 1976). Henri Bonnet wrote an eloquent foreword to this volume, reiterating the themes he had been fighting for since the late 1920s.
15. FO 924/20/LC768, August 18, 1944.
16. Nicholas Spykman, *America's Strategy in World Politics: The United States and the Balance of Power* (New Haven, Conn., 1942), 247–48, 255.
17. FO 924/294, November 29, 1945.
18. Eric Hobsbawm, *The Age of Extremes: A History of the World, 1914–1991* (New York, 1994), ix.

19. F. O. Matthiessen, *From the Heart of Europe* (New York, 1948), 13–14; F. O. Matthiessen, *The Responsibilities of the Critic* (New York, 1952), 13.

20. John Nef, *War and Human Progress: An Essay on the Rise of Industrial Civilization* (New York, 1950), 414.

21. *New Yorker* 25 (June 18, 1949), 74–76; *New Statesman and Nation* 37 (June 18, 1949), 646–48.

22. I am referring to Hobsbawm, *Age of Extremes* and John Grenville, *A History of the World in the Twentieth Century* (Cambridge, Mass., 1994).

23. *Coopération technique,* no. 62 (Paris, 1970): 1.

24. Hartmut Kaelble, "Social History of European Integration," paper presented at a conference on "social change and international affairs," Paris, December 5–6, 1994; John E. Farquharson and Stephen C. Holt, *Europe from Below: An Assessment of Franco-German Popular Contacts* (London, 1975), 65–66, 169.

25. David Hollinger, *In the American Province: Studies in the History and Historiography of Ideas* (Bloomington, Ind., 1985), 69; Reinhold Wagnleitner, *Coca-Colonization and the Cold War: The Cultural Mission of the United States in Austria after the Second World War* (Chapel Hill, N.C., 1995), 6.

26. See Ron Robin, *The Barbed-Wire College: Reeducating German POWs in the United States during World War II* (Princeton, 1995). For an interesting study of German "reeducation" in the French zone of occupation, see Monique Mombert, *Jeunesse et livre en zone française d'occupation, 1945–1949* (Strasbourg, 1995). David Reynolds's *Rich Relations: The American Occupation of Britain, 1942–1945* (New York, 1995) recounts how the presence of U.S. soldiers in wartime Britain transformed the latter's society and culture. The most up-to-date study of wartime U.S. plans for reforming Japan is Rudolf V. A. Janssens, *"What Future for Japan?": U.S. Wartime Planning for the Postwar Era, 1942–1945* (Amsterdam, 1995). These monographs serve to establish connections in the cultural realm between the war and the peace.

27. Elaine Tyler May, *Homeward Bound: American Families in the Cold War Era* (New York, 1988); Stephen Whitfield, *The Culture of the Cold War* (New York, 1922).

28. Hollinger, *American Province,* 69.

29. Henry Luce, *The American Century* (New York, 1941), 24, 29, 31, 33–34.

30. Patrick J. Buchannan to Richard M. Nixon, "Notes for Legislative Leadership Meeting" (February 17, 1990), National Security Archive, Washington, D.C.

31. Frank Ninkovich, *U.S. Information Policy and Cultural Diplomacy* (New York, 1996), 28–29.

32. Amos Kenan, *Israel, A Wasted Victory* (Tel Aviv, 1970), 165, 168.

33. Netanel Lorch, *One Long War: Arab versus Jew since 1920* (Jerusalem, 1978), 12.

34. Kishida Junnosuke, "The Global Management of Technology," paper presented at a conference on "the end of the century," Washington, November 3–5, 1994.

35. Edward Said, *Orientalism* (New York, 1978).

36. Cornelius Castoriadis, "Reflections on 'Rationality' and 'Development'," *Thesis Eleven,* nos. 10/11 (1984/1985): 18–36.

37. John Tomlinson, *Cultural Imperialism: A Critical Introduction* (London, 1991).

38. Hazen Foundation, *Reconstituting the Human Community* (New Haven, 1972), 14, 17.

39. James Davison Hunter, *Culture Wars: The Struggle to Define America* (New York, 1991). A 1995 controversy over an exhibit at the Smithsonian Institution persuaded a publisher to issue a book entitled *History Wars: The Enola Gay and Other Battles for the American Past* (edited by Edward T. Linenthal and Tom Englehardt; New York, 1996). These titles suggest that to some observers wars were no longer interstate conflicts but were domestic fissures. For an extremely thoughtful essay on the emphasis on "the local, the fragmentary, the particular" in the United States, see David Hollinger, "How Wide the Circle of the 'We'? American Intellectuals and the Problem of Ethnos since World War II," *American Historical Review* 98: 317–37 (April 1993).

40. Pierre Bourdieu, *Distinction: A Social Critique of the Judgment of Taste* (Cambridge, Mass., 1984).

41. *Economist,* November 5, 1994: 83.

CONCLUSION:
Toward a Cultural Definition of International Relations

1. See James Der Derian and Michael J. Shapiro, eds., *International/Intertextual Relations* (Lexington, 1989) for examples of a postmodernist approach to international relations.

2. Oscar Handlin, "One World" (Oxford, 1974).

3. H. G. Wells, *The Way to World Peace* (London, 1930), 22.

4. Cited in John T. Trumpbour, "'Death to Hollywood'" (Ph.D. diss., Harvard University, 1996). 364.

5. I found it encouraging that in 1995, even as various governments commemorated the fiftieth anniversary of the ending of World War II, plans were made all over the world to celebrate, in 1996, the fiftieth anniversary of the launching of the Fulbright program. In Europe, the Middle East, Africa, Asia, and Latin America, local Fulbright committees (or their equivalents) cooperated with representatives of the United States Information Service to hold symposia, workshops, exhibits, and concerts to reaffirm their commitment to the principles of cross-cultural communication, mutual understanding, and international cooperation in coping with specific global problems.

INDEX

Library of Congress Cataloging-in-Publication Data

Iriye, Akira.
  Cultural internationalism and world order / Akira Iriye.
      p.   cm.   —   (The Albert Shaw memorial lectures)
  Includes bibliographical references and index.
  ISBN 0-8018-5457-1   (alk. paper)
    1. Civilization, Modern—20th century.   2. Intercultural com-
  munication.   3. Cultural relativism.   I. Title.   II. Series.
D842.I75   1997   96-25160
303.48'2'09041—dc20   CIP